Roadmap to Non-Exec

The Essential

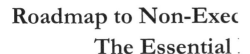

CW00818815

Insights From An International Corporate
Governance And Board Expert

By Taka Sande

Table of Contents

About the Author

Taka Sande, a Certified Director® (IoDSA) and Project Management Professional (PMP)®, brings a wealth of leadership experience in executive management and corporate governance to the table. He offers expert strategic advisory services to private sector organizations, state-owned enterprises, non-profits, and government departments, both locally and on the global stage.

In his capacity as the Managing Director of Fasford Group, Taka also actively serves on various corporate boards, assuming roles as a Non-Executive Director (NED), advisor, or committee member. His contributions span diverse organizations, including private companies, state-owned enterprises, and non-profit entities.

Taka is a versatile professional, doubling as a renowned speaker, mentor, trainer, and consultant specializing in corporate governance, board development, director training, King IV Report, ISO37000, strategy, ethics, and business transformation. His expertise caters to boards of mid to large-sized organizations across the public and private sectors, encompassing start-ups, family businesses, and non-profit organizations. Taka has a track record of corporate governance consulting with companies and organizations in Southern Africa, the United States, Canada, and the Middle East region.

In addition to his numerous qualifications, Taka holds the esteemed title of Project Management Professional (PMP)®, accompanied by a Master of Business Administration (MBA) degree, a BSc Honors in Civil Engineering degree, and a collection of various certificates. He is deeply passionate about advancing your board career development and fostering organizational growth.

Preface

Initially conceived as a brief guide, the evolution of this book has transformed it into a comprehensive resource. Recognizing the need for a more detailed exploration, I decided to cover a broad spectrum of areas and make it a substantial volume.

This book was crafted against the backdrop of a post-COVID world, reflecting the shifts in corporate governance it ushered in. Following the pandemic, significant transformations unfolded across the corporate governance sphere. The ensuing era prompted a profound reassessment of governance norms, highlighting the importance of resilience, diversity within boards, managing economic unpredictability, sustainable practices, adaptive governance approaches, digital integration, cybersecurity measures, transparency, Environmental, Social, and Governance (ESG) considerations, and a renewed focus on stakeholder welfare.

Designed for individuals aspiring to Non-Executive Director (NED) positions, those recently appointed seeking to fortify their foundations, and current NEDs aspiring to expand their portfolio, this book serves as a valuable tool. It offers guidance on navigating the path to a non-executive career, searching for board positions, and excelling in the role of a NED.

While the primary focus is on non-executive career development, the scope extends to executive career growth. This book goes beyond the confines of a typical corporate governance guide, providing insightful advice tailored for board members. The principles outlined within these pages are, thus, not confined to board positions alone; they are equally applicable to executive career advancement.

It's important to note that the guidance offered here is not prescriptive or absolute. Instead, it encourages you to selectively adopt what aligns with your specific context, including factors such as location, culture, career direction, and professional development level. Emphasizing flexibility, this book empowers you to tailor your insights to your unique circumstances, ensuring practical applicability.

1. Introduction

1.1. Background

Many believe that you must spend years as an executive before transitioning to a Non-Executive Director (NED) role later in life. However, this isn't the case. You can develop your NED career alongside your executive career. In fact, the experiences from one can enhance the other.

Securing a spot on a board is an exceptionally competitive pursuit. Interestingly, it is notable that, on average worldwide, each board of directors appoints at least one new member annually. As an aspiring board member, you might be asking, '*Where are they choosing them from?*'

Historically, conventional board appointment methods gave rise to exclusive networks within boardrooms, often biased by gender, race, and background. However, contemporary shifts, propelled by the digital age and evolving corporate governance demands, are reshaping the board appointment environment. These changes have paved the way for emerging talents, offering opportunities for new faces and promising directors to leave their imprint.

The Heidrick & Struggles Board Monitor US 2022 Report, concentrating on Fortune 500 boards, disclosed a significant milestone: 43% of board seats were occupied by first-time directors, marking a historic high. This trend is a direct outcome of evolving board composition imperatives, fuelled by a focused emphasis on:

- Diversity, Equity, and Inclusion (DEI), encompasses diversity in race, gender, age, skills, culture, location, etc.
- Environmental, Social, and Governance (ESG) considerations, including climate change and sustainability.

- The growing demand for information technology governance expertise, especially in response to the escalating prominence of cybersecurity and related domains.
- The impacts of Covid-19. The pandemic-induced slowdown and restrictions compelled boards to reassess and evolve through innovation.
- Age is now becoming irrelevant. Young, excellent directors are being sought. There is a great need for directors who understand the current trends, especially with regard to technology and innovation.

Present trends indicate that board appointments are no longer exclusively reserved for highly experienced senior executives with decades of industry knowledge. These days, any individual possessing the requisite skills and qualifications to fulfill the desired board composition can attain board positions.

The roles of board members have undergone significant transformation. It is no longer confined to mere oversight. Today's board responsibilities encompass vital tasks such as fostering innovation, rigorously evaluating risk management strategies, and spearheading cultural transformation within organizations.

1.2. What Is Corporate Governance?

Let's start right from the beginning by defining 'corporate governance.'

Corporate governance refers to the system of rules, practices, and processes by which an organization is directed and controlled. The King IV Report on Corporate Governance defines corporate governance *as the exercise of ethical and effective leadership by the governing body (board) towards the achievement of the following governance outcomes; ethical culture, good performance, effective control, and legitimacy.*

Corporate governance involves providing oversight and balancing the interests of various stakeholders simultaneously, such as shareholders, management, customers, suppliers, financiers, government, and the community. The primary goal of corporate governance is to ensure the organization operates efficiently, ethically, and in the best interest of all material stakeholders.

Some of the key components of corporate governance include:

- **Board of Directors:** The board of directors is responsible for overseeing the organization's management and ensuring that it acts in the best interest of the organization. It approves key decisions, provides guidance to management, and monitors the organization's performance.

- **Executive Management:** The organization's executive managers are responsible for the day-to-day operations. Corporate governance ensures that management acts in accordance with the organization's objectives and adheres to ethical standards.

- **Shareholders and Investors:** Shareholders are the owners of the company or organization, and corporate governance mechanisms should protect their interests, without excluding other stakeholders. Shareholders typically exercise their influence through voting on key matters and electing members of the board of directors.

- **Transparency and Disclosure:** Organisations are expected to provide timely and accurate information about their financial performance, operations, and decision-making processes. This transparency builds trust among stakeholders.

- **Accountability:** Corporate governance emphasizes accountability, ensuring that those responsible for decision-making are answerable for their actions. This accountability helps prevent abuse of power and promotes responsible behavior.

- **Ethical Behaviour:** Corporate governance encourages ethical conduct in all aspects of an organization's business. This includes fair treatment of employees, honesty in financial reporting, and adherence to laws and regulations.

- **Stakeholder Interests:** Corporate governance considers the interests of various stakeholders, including employees, investors, shareholders, customers, suppliers, creditors, regulators, environmental groups, and the broader community. Balancing these interests helps create a sustainable and responsible business environment.

- **Risk Management:** An effective corporate governance framework includes mechanisms for identifying, assessing, and managing risks. This ensures that the organization is resilient and can navigate challenges effectively.

1.3. The Importance of Sound Corporate Governance

Good corporate governance is essential for the long-term success and sustainability of an organization. It enhances the organization's reputation, attracts investors, and fosters a positive corporate culture. Some countries and regions have specific guidelines and codes of best practices to guide organizations in implementing effective corporate governance.

The role of effective corporate governance cannot be overstated for any organization across the public, private, or the non-profit sector. It stands as a cornerstone influencing your overall performance and reputation. Serving as a vital mechanism, governance ensures that organizations are led responsibly and ethically, thereby safeguarding the interests of shareholders and other stakeholders. The cultivation of trust and confidence among investors, customers, partners, employees, and the industry at large is a direct outcome of sound corporate governance.

At its essence, robust corporate governance places a strong emphasis on transparency and accountability within an organization. Through the implementation of effective governance practices, organizations make a commitment to disclose relevant information about their operations and financial performance. This dedication to open communication empowers shareholders and stakeholders to make well-informed decisions. Moreover, sound corporate governance extends into effective risk management, enhancing an organization's preparedness to face potential challenges and ensuring the protection of the interests of shareholders and stakeholders alike.

1.4. Benefits of Becoming a Non-Executive Director

There are many reasons why you want to become a Non-Executive Director (NED). Some of the reasons may include;

- **Financial Incentive:** While the financial rewards of board positions exist, it's important to note that they are not always guaranteed or substantial. Nevertheless, the potential for additional income remains a motivating factor for many considering NED roles.

- **Escape Boredom and Embrace Change:** Particularly for individuals in mid-career or approaching retirement, serving as a NED provides a welcome shift in responsibilities, offering a dynamic and engaging experience that can eliminate the monotony associated with traditional roles.

- **Philanthropic Impact:** Becoming a NED offers a unique platform to give back to the community. It provides an opportunity to influence positive change, shape organizational strategy, and make substantial contributions beyond the confines of your immediate job role. This philanthropic aspect can be immensely fulfilling.

- **Enjoyment and Excitement:** Serving on boards can be an exhilarating experience. The dynamic nature of boardroom discussions, strategic decision-making, and the overall governance process can inject a sense of excitement into your professional life.

- **Professional Challenge:** Taking on a role as a NED presents a challenge that can broaden your perspective. Learning from a highly experienced and diverse set of individuals exposes you to new ideas and strategies. This challenging environment enhances your critical thinking and deepens your understanding of business intricacies.

- **Personal and Professional Growth:** Embracing a non-executive directorship not only offers personal and professional growth but also strengthens your position as a thought leader. It provides an avenue for expanding your skill set, honing leadership abilities, and contributing to the success of the organization in a more strategic capacity.

- **Networking Opportunities:** In a world where professional connections are paramount, a non-executive directorship positions you among the top leaders in your industry. The networking opportunities inherent in such a role can open doors to collaborations, partnerships, and other avenues for professional advancement.

Considering these multifaceted benefits, becoming a NED emerges as a strategic and rewarding choice for individuals seeking to diversify their professional experiences and contribute meaningfully to organizational success.

1.5. Advantages of Serving as a Voluntary Board Member

When starting a board career, we always recommend starting by serving on a voluntary basis. Considering a role as a voluntary board member offers numerous benefits, some of which may not have crossed your mind. Exploring such opportunities can be a transformative experience with a range of advantages:

- **Professional Skill Development:** Voluntary board service provides a unique chance to hone your professional board skills. The practical application of these skills in a real-world environment not only reinforces your expertise but also allows you to make meaningful contributions to the organization.

- **Learning from Experienced Directors:** Collaborating with more seasoned independent directors offers an invaluable learning experience. Your wealth of experience becomes a valuable resource, providing insights, guidance, and mentorship that can enhance your understanding of effective governance practices.

- **Hidden Opportunities in Non-Profits:** Non-profit organizations often have unadvertised board or committee vacancies due to financial constraints. This creates an environment with less competition for roles, presenting a unique chance for you to step into leadership positions and contribute to the organization's mission.

- **Building Relationships and Expanding Networks:** Serving on a voluntary board allows you to forge connections with individuals who serve on other boards. This interconnected network can open doors to additional board opportunities, as many appointments are not publicly advertised.

- **Contributing to Causes You're Passionate About:** Volunteering on a board provides a distinctive opportunity to work with like-minded individuals and contribute to organizations or causes that align with your passion. This sense of purpose and shared commitment can make your contribution more meaningful.

- **Access to a Supportive Network:** Engaging in voluntary board service exposes you to a new network of people who can support both your professional and board career. These connections can offer advice, mentorship, and valuable insights, contributing to your personal and professional growth.

- **Enhancing Well-Being through Volunteering:** Volunteering with non-profit organizations has been shown to have positive effects on well-being. It can boost social connections, reduce anxiety, improve life satisfaction, offer a sense of purpose, and decrease the risk of depression. This holistic benefit goes beyond the professional domain, impacting your overall quality of life.

Serving as a voluntary board member is not just an opportunity to contribute to a cause; it is a strategic move that can positively impact your professional development, expand your network, and enhance your overall well-being.

Please note that serving on non-profit boards requires passion. The board will look for and demand similar passion from you.

1.6. Preparing Yourself for Board Service

Embarking on a journey as a board member is a significant commitment that requires careful consideration. Before taking on such a responsibility, ask yourself the following questions and assess your readiness for the role:

- **Assessment of Skills and Contributions:** Do you possess the skills and expertise that the boards are seeking? Consider what unique contributions you can bring to the organization based on your professional background and experiences.

- **Alignment with Organizational Interests:** Are you prepared to speak and act in the best interests of the organization? This requires a commitment to making decisions that benefit the organization, even if they may not align with your personal preferences.

- **Tying Your Reputation to the Organization:** Are you prepared to align your reputation with this organization and the livelihoods it sustains? Board members play a crucial role in shaping the organization's image, and their reputations are often intertwined with the success and reputation of the entity.

- **Authentic Passion for the Organization's Cause:** Do you have an authentic passion for the organization and its cause? Genuine enthusiasm and belief in the mission of the organization will drive your commitment and contribution as a board member.

- **Time Commitment:** Do you have the time required to fulfill the responsibilities of the role? Serving on a board involves regular meetings, preparation, and active participation in decision-making processes. Ensure you can dedicate the necessary time to contribute effectively.

- **Understanding of Responsibilities:** Are you aware of the specific responsibilities associated with the role? Familiarize yourself with the duties and expectations of a board member, including legal and ethical obligations.

- **Acceptance of Liability:** Are you ready to take on the associated liability? Board members may bear legal responsibilities for certain decisions and actions taken by the organization. Understand and accept the potential legal implications of the role.

- **Navigating Politics and Passion:** Are you prepared for the politics that may arise when working with passionate individuals? Boards can be dynamic environments with diverse opinions;

readiness to navigate potential conflicts and differing perspectives is crucial.

- **Interest in Serving, Even Unpaid:** Are you interested in serving, even if it's not always a paid role? Board service is often voluntary, and individuals are driven by a desire to contribute to a cause rather than monetary compensation.

- **Consideration of the Right Timing:** Is this the right time for your professional and board career? Assess whether your current professional commitments align with the demands of board service and whether the timing is conducive to your overall career goals.

As an aspiring NED, you should carefully reflect on these considerations to ensure you are fully prepared and committed to the responsibilities that come with serving on a board.

2.1. Introduction

Embarking on a Non-Executive Director (NED) career necessitates a foundational focus on self-awareness that translates into the formulation of a personal strategy. The bedrock of a robust board career lies in the ability to comprehend oneself, understand your value, and strategically position yourself. Leaders who are at the corporate level – who lack self-awareness, social awareness, and an understanding of their intrinsic value and leadership style – often exhibit shortcomings in governance, posing risks to their career progression and the organizations they lead. Some organizations find it imperative to send their executives for training, particularly following a comprehensive 360-degree self-awareness evaluation.

By establishing a solid foundation in these areas, you can extend your focus to social awareness and social mastery. This, in turn, forms the basis for mastering skills, comprehending, and delivering value through your expertise, and achieving leadership and governance mastery.

This section aims to equip you with foundational practical tips and strategies to begin navigating your journey towards excellence in leadership and governance. To do so, we will use the three phases of self-awareness.

2.2. Phase 1: Fostering Self-Awareness and Personal Development

The initial phase of self-awareness and personal development, inspired by Coleman's Model, is a critical foundation for individuals aspiring to excel in leadership. This stage is delineated into four quadrants, with the first two emphasizing personal growth and development and the subsequent two focusing on social connectedness.

Coleman's Model – a look at the elements of each quadrant.

1. **Self-Awareness:** According to the Oxford Language Dictionary, self-awareness is defined as "conscious knowledge of one's own character, feelings, motives, and desires." It encompasses several key components: emotional self-awareness, which involves recognizing and understanding one's emotions; accurate self-awareness, which refers to the ability to accurately perceive values, emotions, behaviors, and motivations; and self-confidence, which is the assurance in understanding oneself and recognizing the origin and impact of one's values, emotions, and behaviors on others.

2. **Self-Management:** Strengthening self-awareness provides the foundation for effective self-management, which is the ability to regulate behaviors, thoughts, and emotions. Key aspects of self-management include self-control, the capacity to manage impulses and emotions, fostering composure and resilience; transparency, acting with openness and honesty in both personal and professional interactions; adaptability, the ability to adjust to changing circumstances; being achievement-driven, a commitment to pursuing and reaching personal and professional goals; and initiative, the proactive willingness to take responsibility and action.

3. **Social Awareness:** Improving self-management can enhance social awareness, which is the ability to understand and consider the perspectives of individuals, groups, or communities and apply this understanding in interactions. Social awareness involves empathy, the ability to understand and share the feelings of others, fostering deeper connections; cognitive flexibility, the capacity to adjust perspectives and comprehend different viewpoints; organizational awareness, the understanding of social dynamics and structures within an organization; and service orientation, a commitment to recognizing and meeting the needs of others.

4. **Relationship Management:** The foundation of strong relationships is rooted in heightened self-awareness. Relationship management, in essence, is the art of influencing people to become the best versions of themselves. It involves teamwork and collaboration, working effectively with others to achieve shared goals; building bonds, creating meaningful connections that enhance a positive organizational culture; conflict management, skilfully resolving disputes; persuasion, using effective communication to influence others; acting as a change catalyst, fostering an environment that encourages positive transformation; and inspiring, influencing, and developing others, guiding them toward growth and success. Additionally, it requires a keen understanding of organizational dynamics.

Better self-management is a product of better self-awareness. You must know yourself and know your behavior to manage yourself better. Better relationship management comes from better social awareness. You must be aware and sensitive to the social environment around you to manage relationships effectively. On the other hand, your social awareness is enhanced by your self-awareness.

By progressing through these dimensions of self-awareness and personal development, you not only fortify your own foundational skills but also cultivate the essential attributes required for effective leadership. This holistic approach sets the stage for the next section, where these foundational elements are further refined and applied in the context of leadership and governance mastery.

2.3. Phase 2: Crafting Your Value Creation Model

In the second stage of personal and professional development (also called the intermediate level), we look at the concept of Value Creation, focusing on individual and team value creation. This stage not only amplifies your personal value proposition but also emphasizes the synergy required for effective team dynamics.

1. **Individual Value Creation:** Individual value creation is about understanding how you generate value through your skills, capabilities, and experiences. This concept is reflected in your personal value proposition, a statement that clearly defines your unique value and how you can benefit an organization, project, or role.

   A key aspect of this is identifying your capabilities and value offerings, recognizing the strengths, skills, and expertise that form the core of your value proposition. From there, it's important to optimize your value by striving for excellence and fully leveraging your abilities. Achievement orientation plays a crucial role, as it involves fostering a mindset focused on setting and reaching ambitious goals.

   Self-empowerment is another essential factor, requiring you to take ownership of your personal development and empower yourself to overcome challenges and succeed. Being results-oriented ensures that your efforts are directed toward achieving tangible outcomes and accomplishments, aligning both with your own and the organization's objectives.

2. **Value Creation in a Team:** An enhanced understanding of your personal value creation empowers you to contribute more effectively to team efforts. By recognizing your own strengths and capabilities, you can work towards team goals by developing the skills necessary to collaborate seamlessly with others, ensuring that everyone's efforts align toward achieving collective objectives.

   Agility becomes essential in this process, as embracing adaptability and flexibility allows the team to respond efficiently to changing circumstances. Collaboration plays a crucial role, fostering an environment where teamwork thrives and diverse skills and perspectives are integrated for maximum impact.

Recognizing diversity as a tool for performance is key, as it highlights the value of diverse talents within the team, viewing them as assets that enhance overall performance. Value creation in diversity acknowledges that a team made up of varied perspectives, skills, and approaches leads to greater creativity and innovation. As such, leveraging agility, collaboration, and diversity helps to elevate the team's overall performance.

The team's value creation is dependent on each team member's understanding of their personal value creation. The team's value is simply the collective value of each individual team member. You choose team members who understand their individual values. Usually, your compelling personal value proposition is formed from your understanding of your individual values.

Understanding and honing both personal and team value-creation capabilities are pivotal for you to contribute meaningfully to the board of directors.

2.4. Phase 3: Defining Your Leadership Style

As we progress into the third stage of personal and professional development, we look at the crucial aspect of leadership style. This stage unfolds in two dimensions: executive leadership and governance mastery, each integral to shaping effective leaders in corporate governance.

1. **Executive Leadership:** Leading, influencing, and inspiring others involves developing the ability to guide individuals toward the achievement of shared goals and objectives. This also includes honing coaching and mentoring skills to empower team members and support their growth and professional development. Leveraging the collective strengths and resources within the team, therefore, helps leaders to optimize performance. Additionally, mastering effective communication is crucial for conveying visions, strategies, and expectations clearly and impactfully.

2. **Governance Mastery:** Your executive leadership capabilities provide a strong foundation for mastering governance principles. Ethical and effective governance involves leading with transparency, integrity, and accountability, ensuring decisions are made in the best interest of the organization. Approaching governance with diligence and independence is key, requiring a thorough examination of the main issues and maintaining impartiality in decision-making.

   Strategic governance focuses on guiding the organization in developing strategies that align with long-term goals and stakeholder interests. Policy governance plays a major role in crafting and implementing policies that govern the organization's activities, mitigating risks, and ensuring compliance with regulations.

   Performance governance ensures the organization's success by setting performance metrics, monitoring progress, and driving continuous improvement. Additionally, reporting governance emphasizes the importance of accurate and transparent reporting mechanisms that give stakeholders a clear and comprehensive view of the organization's activities and outcomes.

Understanding and perfecting your leadership style is vital when performing at executive leadership and governance level. In the next section, we will look at practical insights and strategies that will aid you in refining your leadership approach and fortifying your role as an influential leader in the boardroom.

2.5. Tools for Self-Awareness and Personal Strategy

There are several well-known self-awareness assessments and tests that individuals and organizations use worldwide. Here are some of the top ones:

1. **Myers-Briggs Type Indicator (MBTI):** A widely used personality test that categorizes individuals into one of 16 personality types based on preferences related to how they perceive the world and make decisions.

2. **DISC Assessment:** Focuses on four personality traits: Dominance, Influence, Steadiness, and Conscientiousness. It helps you understand your behavior in various situations.

3. **Emotional Intelligence Appraisal (EQ-i 2.0):** Measures emotional intelligence, assessing factors such as self-perception, interpersonal relationships, stress management, and decision-making.

4. **StrengthsFinder (now CliftonStrengths):** Identifies an individual's top strengths out of a list of 34, providing insights into areas where they naturally excel.

5. **Enneagram Personality Test:** Classifies individuals into one of nine personality types, offering insights into motivations, fears, and areas for personal and professional growth.

6. **Hogan Assessments:** Includes various assessments that measure personality, values, and motives, providing insights into how individuals approach work and interpersonal relationships.

7. **FIRO-B (Fundamental Interpersonal Relations Orientation-Behaviour):** Assesses an individual's interpersonal needs and behaviors, focusing on areas such as inclusion, control, and affection.

8. **Strengths-based Leadership Assessment:** Expands on the StrengthsFinder concept, focusing on strengths specifically related to leadership styles and approaches.

9. **360-Degree Feedback:** A multi-rater assessment where you receive feedback from various sources, including peers, subordinates, and supervisors, providing a comprehensive view of your performance.

10. **The Leadership Circle Profile:** Evaluates leadership effectiveness and potential by measuring creative and reactive leadership competencies.

It's important to note that the effectiveness of these assessments can vary, and individuals may resonate differently with different tools. Additionally, the context in which these assessments are used, and the interpretation of results, can significantly impact your value. Always consider consulting with qualified professionals when using these assessments for personal or organizational development.

2.6. Developing Your Career Strategy

The process of developing a career strategy requires the results from your self-awareness assessments, your value-creating assessments, and your leadership style.

Embarking on a successful career requires more than just going through the motions of day-to-day work. It demands a deliberate and thoughtful approach in the form of a career strategy that guides your actions, decisions, and aspirations. Thus, developing a well-defined career plan, setting SMART goals, and understanding the resources involved help you to continuously navigate your professional journey with purpose and intentionality.

1) Developing the Career Plan

A robust career plan serves as the roadmap for your professional journey, outlining clear objectives and milestones, covering the entire career trajectory, often across different roles, industries, or stages of professional life. The components include:

- Long-term career goals (e.g., becoming a senior executive, transitioning into a new industry).
- Potential career paths and opportunities.
- Major milestones such as promotions, job changes, or entering new fields.
- Strategies to align personal values and aspirations with professional goals.

It typically spans short-term, medium-term, and long-term goals, providing a structured approach to career development.

- **Short-Term Goals (3 months to a year):** Setting short-term goals allows you to focus on immediate actions that contribute to your overall career progression. These objectives should be achievable within a relatively brief timeframe and serve as stepping stones for larger aspirations.

- **Medium-Term Goals (1 to 3 years):** Medium-term goals bridge the gap between short-term achievements and long-term aspirations. They often involve acquiring specific skills, gaining experience, or assuming roles that contribute to your professional growth.

- **Master Dream List (5 years from now):** Envisioning your career five years into the future helps create a comprehensive roadmap. The master dream list involves outlining your ultimate career aspirations and providing a long-term vision that informs your strategic decisions.

Your career plan must outline a vision for your career, mapping out long-term goals, potential career paths, and major milestones over several years or decades. It emphasizes the overall direction rather than specific skill development. Details of the stages of the career plan are covered by your Professional development plan and your leadership development plan.

2) Developing a Comprehensive Life Strategy

Life is a multifaceted journey, and achieving holistic fulfillment requires a comprehensive approach. A Comprehensive Life Strategy, encompassing various dimensions of well-being, is instrumental in fostering balance, purpose, and success. This holistic perspective involves carefully crafting plans for health, family, career, finances, intellect, spirituality, social connections, and other aspects to ensure a well-rounded and meaningful existence.

1. **Health Plan:** Prioritizing physical well-being is foundational to a Comprehensive Life Strategy. This includes setting fitness goals, adopting a balanced diet, ensuring regular medical check-ups, and cultivating healthy lifestyle habits. Nurturing your body is the cornerstone for sustained energy and vitality in all areas of life.

2. **Family Plan:** Family forms the core support structure in life. A Family Plan involves defining roles, expectations, and shared goals within the family unit. It also includes spending quality time with loved ones, fostering open communication, and creating a nurturing environment that promotes the well-being of each family member.

3. **Career (and Business Plan):** Career aspirations and entrepreneurial pursuits contribute significantly to your sense of purpose and achievement. A Career and Business Plan involves setting professional goals, charting a career trajectory, and identifying opportunities for growth and advancement. This plan aligns personal passions with professional endeavors, ensuring fulfillment in the workplace.

4. **Financial Plan:** Financial stability is a crucial component of a well-rounded life. A Financial Plan encompasses budgeting, savings, investments, and long-term financial goals. It provides a roadmap for managing resources, minimizing financial stress, and building a secure foundation for future endeavors.

5. **Intellect and Mental Plan:** This plan covers Mindset and Beliefs. Developing mental resilience and fostering a growth mindset is integral to personal development. The intellect and mental plan involves continuous learning, challenging limiting beliefs and cultivating a positive mindset. This plan supports intellectual growth and emotional well-being.

6. **Spiritual Plan:** Nurturing the spiritual dimension of life provides a sense of purpose and inner peace. A Spiritual Plan involves practices such as meditation, reflection, and engaging in activities that align with personal beliefs. It fosters a connection to something greater than oneself and contributes to overall well-being.

7. **Social and Connectedness:** This plan includes the Friendships, Advisors & Mentors Plan. Building and maintaining meaningful connections with others is essential for a fulfilling life. The Social Plan includes cultivating friendships, seeking guidance from advisors, and engaging with mentors. These relationships contribute to personal growth, provide support, and enrich the social fabric of life.

8. **Other Plans:** The "Other Plans" encompasses any additional dimensions or goals that are unique to an individual's aspirations. This might include hobbies, travel plans, or personal projects that bring joy and fulfillment.

A Comprehensive Life Strategy is a roadmap for living a purposeful, balanced, and fulfilled life. By addressing various aspects, from health and family to career, finances, and beyond, you can create a holistic framework that guides your actions and decisions. This intentional approach to life planning fosters resilience, adaptability, and a sense of purpose, contributing to a rich and meaningful existence.

2.7. Resources and Costs to Consider

Every career plan comes with resource implications, and understanding these costs is crucial for effective planning and execution.

- **Skills and Development:** Acquiring new skills or enhancing existing ones is an investment in your professional growth. Identify the skills required for your career goals and allocate time and resources for continuous learning and development.

- **Time:** Time is a valuable resource, and managing it effectively is essential. Consider the time commitment required for skill acquisition, networking, and other career-building activities. Prioritize tasks and create a schedule that aligns with your goals.

- **Financial:** Some career advancements may involve financial investments, such as certifications, courses, or conferences. Budgeting for these expenses ensures you're financially prepared for opportunities that contribute to your career strategy.

- **Personal and Professional (Friends, Advisors, Mentors):** Building a support network is a critical resource. Friends, advisors, and mentors provide guidance, insights, and networking opportunities. Cultivate meaningful professional relationships to enrich your career journey.

- **SMART Goals:** Incorporating the SMART criteria (Specific, Measurable, Achievable, Relevant, Time-bound) into your goal setting ensures that objectives are well-defined and attainable.

28

SMART goals provide clarity, making it easier to track progress and adjust your strategy as needed.

Developing your career strategy is a dynamic and ongoing process that requires intentional planning and execution. By setting SMART goals, understanding the resources involved, and actively pursuing your career plan, you position yourself for success and fulfillment in your professional endeavors. Remember, a well-thought-out strategy not only guides your present actions but also shapes your future achievements.

How is this relevant for a NED or aspiring NED? As a board member, your 360° wellness is important. Challenges in one area will usually spill over and affect your wellness and performance as a board member. A well-balanced life is a great foundation on which to build a successful and fulfilling board career.

3.1. Titles Used for Board of Director Positions

The structure and nomenclature of board of director positions or board positions play a crucial role in defining the roles and responsibilities of individuals entrusted with steering the direction of organizations. Board titles not only reflect the diverse functions within governing bodies but also emphasize the specific nature of each role. Let's look at some of the titles associated with board positions.

- **Non-Executive Director (NED):** NEDs bring an external perspective to the board. They are not involved in the day-to-day operations and are crucial for impartial decision-making. Independent Non-Executive Director (INED), as the name suggests, emphasizes an additional layer of autonomy and objectivity, ensuring a balanced governance structure.

- **Board Member:** The generic term "Board Member" encompasses individuals who hold various positions within the board. Board members collectively contribute to strategic decision-making, policy formulation, and organizational oversight. The title is broad, reflecting the diversity of roles and functions within the board.

- **Council Member:** Council Members often serve on boards overseeing specific sectors or areas within an organization. The title implies a collaborative approach to governance, highlighting the collective responsibility of council members in shaping policies and strategies.

- **Trustee (for a Board of Trustees):** Trustees, typically associated with non-profit organizations, hold a fiduciary responsibility to ensure the organization's resources are used in alignment with its mission. The title emphasizes a duty of care towards the organization's beneficiaries and stakeholders.

- **Committee or Subcommittee Member:** Boards often form committees or subcommittees to address specific functions or areas such as audit, compensation, or governance. Committee or Subcommittee Members focus on in-depth analysis and decision-making within their designated spheres, contributing to the overall efficacy of the board.

The variety of titles for board positions reflects the multifaceted nature of governance structures and the diverse skills needed for effective leadership. While NEDs bring an external and independent perspective, board members collectively contribute to the overarching goals of the organization. Council Members emphasize collaboration, and Trustees hold a distinctive responsibility in the realm of non-profit governance. Committee or Subcommittee Members focus on specialized areas, ensuring thorough examination and decision-making.

The choice of board titles is deliberate, aligning with the specific roles and responsibilities each position entails. Understanding the differences between these titles is essential for both board members and stakeholders, fostering transparency and clarity in the governance hierarchy. Each title, with its unique connotations, contributes to the variety of expertise and leadership required for sound and effective governance.

3.2. Advisory Board Vs. Board of Directors

Both Advisory Boards and Boards of Directors play pivotal roles, yet their structures, functions, and responsibilities diverge significantly. Using each title correctly is crucial for organizations seeking to enhance their strategic guidance, decision-making processes, and overall effectiveness.

1) Advisory Board

An Advisory Board represents a less formal association of individuals who contribute their expertise and insights to guide an organization's leadership. Unlike the Board of Directors, members of an Advisory Board do not carry fiduciary or legal responsibilities towards the owners or shareholders. This distinction liberates you from the binding requirements of regular board meetings, offering a more flexible and consultative framework.

Key Characteristics:
- *Informal Nature:* The Advisory Board operates with a more relaxed and informal structure, fostering open communication and a collaborative environment.
- *No Fiduciary Responsibility:* Members are not burdened with legal obligations, allowing them to focus solely on providing advice, feedback, and mentorship.
- *Limited Decision-Making Involvement:* While Advisory Board members offer guidance, they are typically not directly involved in the decision-making processes of the organization.

Suited for:
- *Early-Stage Entrepreneurs and Start-ups:* Advisory Boards are particularly beneficial for emerging ventures seeking mentorship and strategic insights without the stringent governance structures associated with larger corporations.

2) Board of Directors

In contrast, a Board of Directors is a formal governing body that holds ultimate power and carries fiduciary and legal responsibilities on behalf of the organization. This board is fully accountable to the owners and shareholders, making decisions that directly impact the organization's direction and performance. Regular meetings and active involvement in decision-making processes characterize the governance dynamics of a Board of Directors.

Key Characteristics:
- *Fiduciary and Legal Responsibilities:* Directors are legally obligated to act in the best interests of the organization, its shareholders, and other stakeholders, holding a significant level of accountability.
- *Regular Meetings:* Boards of Directors conduct regular meetings to deliberate on critical matters, ensuring ongoing oversight and strategic alignment.
- *Stringent Compliance Structures:* Boards adhere to rigorous compliance structures and systems, upholding governance standards and ensuring regulatory requirements are met.

Suited for:
- *Organizations Seeking Decision-Makers:* Boards of Directors are ideal for organizations that require a formalized governance structure with individuals who not only provide advice but are actively involved in the decision-making processes.

While both Advisory Boards and Boards of Directors contribute to organizational growth, they serve distinct purposes and are best suited for different stages of an organization's development. Advisory Boards offer flexibility, mentorship, and advice, making them valuable for start-ups. On the other hand, Boards of Directors bring formal governance, legal accountability, and decision-making expertise, making them indispensable for established organizations dealing with complex business environments. Ultimately, the choice between the two depends on the specific needs, goals, and developmental stage of the organization.

3.3. Types of Directors

The role of directors is pivotal in shaping the direction and success of an organization. Directors bring diverse skills, perspectives, and responsibilities to the boardroom, contributing to the holistic functioning of the organization. Let's look into the various types of directors, each with its distinctive roles, responsibilities, and characteristics.

- **Executive Director:** An Executive Director is typically a senior executive within the organization, often holding a C-level position. They are actively involved in the day-to-day operations and strategic decision-making, bridging the gap between management and the board.

- **Non-Executive Director (NED):** NEDs do not have a full-time executive role within the organization. They bring external perspectives, providing independent insights and oversight. NEDs contribute to strategic discussions and decision-making without being directly involved in daily operations.

- **Independent Non-Executive Director (INED):** INEDs are free from any material relationships with the organization that could compromise their objectivity. They play a key role in providing unbiased viewpoints, particularly in matters of strategy, risk, and executive remuneration.

- **Lead Independent Non-executive Director:** The Lead Independent Non-Executive Director is appointed when the Chairman faces conflicts of interest, allowing them to assume a leadership role if the Chairman is not independent. Their primary responsibility is to provide guidance and leadership to the board in situations where the Chairman is conflicted, while ensuring the Chairman's authority remains intact. The board may also assign the roles of Lead Independent Director and Deputy Chairman to the same individual.

- **Nominee/Representative Director:** An individual who is appointed to a company's board to represent another person or entity, fulfilling legal and regulatory requirements. The entity is usually a shareholder, an investor, a creditor or financial institution, or any other third party.

- **Alternate/Shadow Director:** An Alternate or Shadow Director is appointed by a director to represent them in their absence. While they assume the director's responsibilities temporarily, the original director retains the legal and fiduciary obligations associated with the position.

- **Temporary/Interim Director:** The board of directors has the authority to appoint an individual who meets the qualifications for election as a director to fill a vacancy on a temporary basis. This appointment typically continues until the vacancy is permanently filled through election by shareholders. The company's memorandum of incorporation may prohibit such temporary appointments.

- **Ex-officio Director:** An Ex-officio Director holds a position on the board by virtue of their position in another organization, often an affiliated entity. This type of directorship is tied to a specific role or office, granting automatic board membership.

3.4. The Value of NEDs

The inclusion of NEDs has been consistently proven to be a catalyst for positive change, yielding tangible benefits for both private and public organizations. Countless studies underscore the transformative impact that NEDs bring to corporate and financial performance, making their role indispensable in steering organizations toward sustainable success.

- **Expertise in Specialized Areas:** NEDs are a repository of specialized expertise, boasting extensive industry knowledge, hands-on experience, and strategic acumen. Their contribution transcends traditional boundaries, providing invaluable insights when evaluating business strategies, assessing risks, and making well-informed decisions. The diversity in their perspectives serves as a catalyst for innovation, challenging existing paradigms and elevating the quality of decision-making processes.

- **Objective and Independent Advice:** An inherent strength of NEDs lies in their ability to offer objective advice derived from an independent standpoint. Unaffiliated with the organization's management or controlling shareholders, they bring an unbiased lens to board discussions. This independence is a formidable defense against groupthink, ensuring that decisions align resolutely with the best interests of the organization and its stakeholders.

- **Enhanced Credibility:** The mere presence of NEDs elevates the credibility of a business. Their distinguished reputation and external perspectives instil confidence among investors, customers, and stakeholders at large. This heightened trust in governance practices cultivates stronger relationships with external entities, fostering an environment conducive to sustained growth.

- **Access to Valuable Networks:** Beyond their individual expertise, NEDs provide an invaluable gateway to expansive professional networks. These networks, cultivated over years of experience, serve as conduits to potential partnerships, collaborations, and lucrative business opportunities. Moreover, they play a pivotal role in talent acquisition, facilitate access to capital markets, and offer unparalleled industry insights, enhancing the strategic positioning of the organization.

- **Mitigation of Conflicts and Promotion of Transparency:** Notably, NEDs navigate boardroom dynamics with fewer conflicts of interest compared to their insider counterparts. This independence acts as a safeguard against self-serving behaviors, fostering transparency in deliberations and decision-making. It ensures a balanced distribution of power within the board, culminating in strategic decisions that align seamlessly with the long-term interests of the organization and its shareholders.

The multifaceted contributions of NEDs extend far beyond conventional governance paradigms. Their expertise, independence, networks, and commitment to transparency collectively weave a narrative of enhanced corporate governance, propelling organizations toward resilience, innovation, and sustained success.

3.5. The Board's Key Governance Duties

The board of directors, comprising both Executive and Non-Executive Directors, provides oversight and steers the organization's strategic direction. The responsibilities entrusted to the Board extend far beyond mere oversight, encompassing a spectrum of strategic, ethical, and legal dimensions. The board of directors must act in the best interest of the organization; this includes sustainability in the context of corporate citizenship. The composition of the board, the role of the board chair, independence, expertise, and decision-making processes are pivotal elements contributing to effective corporate governance.

Understanding the pivotal role of the board in corporate governance is essential for establishing and maintaining effective governance practices within organizations. The board of directors bears key governance responsibilities and duties, including:

- **Focal Point of Corporate Governance:** The Board stands as the central pillar of corporate governance, orchestrating the governance level. It is the epicenter where accountability, transparency, and ethical conduct converge. The Board sets the tone for organizational behavior and establishes a governance framework that aligns with the organization's values and objectives.

- **Setting Direction and Tone:** An overarching responsibility of the Board is to set the organizational compass, defining the direction and tone that permeate the entire entity. This involves articulating a compelling vision, establishing core values, and fostering a culture that resonates with stakeholders. The Board's influence in shaping the organizational ethos is pivotal for long-term success.

- **Approval of Strategy, Policy, and Business Planning:** Strategic decision-making resides at the core of the Board's responsibilities. The approval of overarching strategies, policies, and business plans falls within its purview. Through rigorous deliberations, the Board ensures that these elements are not only aligned with the organization's mission but also responsive to dynamic market conditions and stakeholder expectations.

- **CEO Appointment and Succession Planning:** The appointment of a Chief Executive Officer (CEO) is a critical juncture where the Board exercises its governance duties. Furthermore, the Board takes a proactive role in succession planning, ensuring a seamless transition in leadership. This involves identifying and developing talent within the organization to sustain a robust leadership pipeline.

- **Overseeing Implementation and Execution:** Beyond strategic formulation, the Board is actively engaged in overseeing the implementation and execution of approved plans. This involves regular assessments of operational performance, risk management, and compliance with relevant laws and regulations. The Board's vigilance ensures that strategic objectives are translated into tangible results, safeguarding the organization's trajectory.

- **Directors' Legal Duties:** Directors are entrusted with legal duties that encompass both joint and personal liability. This legal framework underscores the accountability directors bear toward the organization. It is a commitment to act in the best interests of the organization, avoiding conflicts of interest, and upholding legal and ethical standards.

- **Individual Director's Duty to the Organization:** Each director assumes a distinct duty to the organization. This personalized obligation mandates directors to act with diligence, prudence, and loyalty. Your decisions and actions collectively shape the corporate destiny, and each director bears the responsibility for contributing to the organization's success.

- Establishing board committees, such as audit and compensation committees, to oversee specific functions, and advisory boards or committees for guidance. Serving as a liaison between shareholders and management.

In essence, the governance duties of the Board form the bedrock of organizational resilience and sustainability. The intricate interplay of strategic direction, ethical oversight, legal adherence, and individual accountability sets the stage for a governance framework that not only meets regulatory standards but propels the organization toward excellence and longevity.

3.6. What Is The Ideal Board Size?

The size of corporate boards can vary widely and is subject to change based on organization policies, regulations, and other factors. Additionally, specific data on the average board size may not be consistently available for all regions and countries. Board sizes are influenced by the organization's structure, industry, and corporate governance practices.

Average board sizes of well-resourced organizations can go up to 10 members. Meanwhile, in limitedly resourced and smaller organizations, the average number is 5-6 members.

3.7. Pathways To the Boardroom

The journey to the boardroom is as diverse as the individuals who embark upon it. The avenues leading to a board position are manifold, reflecting a rich tapestry of expertise, experience, and personal connections. This section illuminates the various routes to the boardroom, offering insights into the different pathways that you traverse in your pursuit of governance roles.

1) Invitation to Board:
- *Based on Expertise:* Individuals possessing exceptional expertise, knowledge, or skills in specialized domains, be it academia, forensic accounting, data science, nuclear research, artificial intelligence, or other niche areas, may receive invitations to join a board. This is a testament to the value your unique perspectives bring to governance discussions.
- *Representative:* Board invitations may also be extended based on an individual's association, such as organizational representation or involvement in a family business. This route emphasizes the significance of an individual's affiliations and the value they bring to the boardroom through diverse connections.

2) Entry at Organisation Start-up Stage
- *Founders or First Board:* You may enter the boardroom at the inception of an organization, contributing to its growth trajectory. This pathway is applicable to both profit and non-profit entities, offering opportunities for visionaries to shape governance structures from the organizational outset.
- *Direct Approach:* Proactive individuals can initiate their journey to the boardroom by directly approaching organizations at the start-up stage with an offer to serve. This self-driven approach

underscores the importance of personal agency and a clear articulation of the value one brings to the governance table.

3) Normal Recruitment

- *Advertised Board Positions:* Board positions may be filled through normal recruitment processes, whether publicly advertised or not. Individuals interested in such roles can actively monitor opportunities and engage in the application process, showcasing their qualifications and alignment with the organization's needs. Responding to advertised board opportunities is a conventional pathway. You can demonstrate your interest and suitability by aligning your skills and experience with the requirements outlined in the advertisement.

- *Board Recruiters:* Board recruiters who specialize in board appointments play a pivotal role in connecting individuals with suitable governance opportunities. As a board candidate, you may leverage the expertise of recruiters to navigate the recruitment process and enhance your visibility in the market.

4) A Combination of the Above

- Many individuals traverse a journey to the boardroom that combines elements of the aforementioned routes. This holistic approach may involve a blend of specialized invitations, proactive engagement with start-ups, active participation in recruitment processes, and collaboration with recruiters to amplify opportunities.

Driven by your expertise, connections, and proactive initiatives, you should navigate these diverse routes to the boardroom. Understanding and embracing this diversity is essential for individuals earnestly seeking to build a dynamic board career.

3.8. What Are The Top Expertise Currently Required by Boards?

A board of directors benefits greatly from a diverse set of expertise among its members. The following key areas of expertise are particularly sought after for individuals considering board member positions:

- **Financial Accounting:** Proficiency in financial accounting, including qualifications such as being a Chartered Accountant and experience in financial audit.
- **Information Technology:** Expertise in information technology, encompassing skills in IT auditing, cybersecurity, artificial intelligence, and IT governance.
- **Human Resources:** Experience in human resources management, demonstrating a comprehensive understanding of HR practices.
- **Investment and Assets Management:** Proficient knowledge in investment strategies and effective assets management.
- **Merger and Acquisition:** Experience in navigating the complexities of mergers and acquisitions, showcasing a strategic understanding of these processes.
- **Business Growth Leadership:** The ability to drive business growth to a mature level, demonstrating strategic leadership skills.
- **International and Multicultural Experience:** Exposure to international business environments and a multicultural perspective, fostering a global outlook.
- **Sector-Specific Expertise:** In-depth knowledge and experience in specific sectors, such as Built Environment, Non-profit, Mining & Engineering, Food Chain Management (FCM), Professional Services, Education and Training, among others.

These diverse areas of expertise contribute to a well-rounded and effective board, ensuring a comprehensive approach to corporate governance in today's dynamic business environment.

3.9. Desired Board Member Attributes

The selection of board members is a pivotal process that requires careful consideration of a myriad of attributes. When searching for individuals to join a board, a comprehensive evaluation encompassing the following general attributes is imperative. These attributes are also included in the job specification:

- **Governance Experience:** An essential criterion for potential board members is a robust background in governance. Previous experience in board roles equips you with the necessary insights into fiduciary duties, regulatory compliance, and effective decision-making processes.

- **Industry and Sector Knowledge:** In-depth knowledge of the industry and sector in which the organization operates is invaluable. Board members with a keen understanding of market trends, competitive landscapes, and industry-specific challenges are better positioned to guide strategic decision-making.

- **Relevant Skills and Experience:** The possession of skills and experiences directly relevant to the organization's needs is a fundamental consideration. Board members should bring a diverse set of skills, ranging from financial acumen and legal expertise to technological proficiency and marketing insight, depending on the organization's requirements.

- **Relevant Qualifications:** Academic and professional qualifications that align with the organization's objectives and challenges are crucial. These qualifications serve as a testament to a board member's expertise and provide a foundation for contributing meaningfully to governance discussions.

- **Adding Diversity:** Embracing diversity in board composition is not just a contemporary trend but a strategic imperative. Boards benefit from diverse perspectives, backgrounds, and experiences, leading to more robust decision-making and a broader understanding of stakeholder needs. However, the board chair is usually skeptical about diversity due to the possibility of disharmony that comes with it.

- **Independence:** Independence is a cornerstone attribute for effective corporate governance. As a Board member, you should be able to exercise independent judgment, free from undue influence, conflicts of interest, or external pressures that could compromise your commitment to the organization's best interests.

- **Availability of Time:** You must have the capacity to commit the necessary time to fulfill your responsibilities effectively. Understanding and aligning with the time demands of board service is crucial for maintaining the board's operational efficiency and effectiveness.

- **Demonstrable Passion:** Beyond mere competence, board members should exhibit a genuine passion for the entity and its mission. Passionate individuals are more likely to invest the time and energy required for a deep understanding of the organization's goals and challenges.

- **Personal and Professional Connections:** A well-connected board member can significantly benefit the organization. Networks of personal and professional connections can facilitate resource mobilization, strategic partnerships, and a broader understanding of industry dynamics.

Each of these attributes contributes to the creation of a well-rounded and effective board of directors. By carefully considering and balancing these factors, organizations can assemble a board that not only possesses the requisite expertise but also reflects the diversity, independence, and passion necessary for successful corporate governance.

3.10.   What Are The Personal Attributes to Look for?

Let's look into the multifaceted qualities that should be sought after when identifying prospective board members. These are observed and assessed through due diligence, pre-interview, during, and post-interview.

- **Commitment to the Organisation:** Deep commitment to do the right thing for shareholders, employees, customers, and stakeholders. A NED must maintain a deep commitment to acting in the best interest of all stakeholders involved. This includes prioritizing the long-term value for shareholders, ensuring the well-being and growth of employees, delivering fair and exceptional service to customers, and considering the broader impacts on the community and other stakeholders. This holistic approach to governance helps balance short-term financial objectives with sustainable, ethical business practices.

- **Support the Executive:** Provide support, encouragement, and value-add to the executive team: A NED plays a crucial role in offering strategic guidance and encouragement to the executive team, acting as a trusted advisor rather than a day-to-day manager. Their primary contribution lies in providing objective insights and drawing from their experience to challenge the leadership constructively. Effectively, their fresh, independent perspective adds significant value to decision-making processes, helping the executive team avoid pitfalls, seize opportunities, and drive long-term business growth.

- **Independent of Harmful Ties:** A paramount consideration in selecting board members is their freedom from harmful associations. Ensuring that you are not entangled in conflicts of interest or questionable affiliations is vital for maintaining the integrity and credibility of the board.

- **Integrity:** Unquestionable integrity is a cornerstone attribute for board members. Those who exhibit a commitment to ethical conduct, transparency, and honesty contribute to a culture of trust within the boardroom and across the organization.

- **Curiosity-Driven:** Inquisitiveness is a trait that distinguishes effective board members. Individuals with a natural curiosity are inclined to investigate into complex issues, ask probing questions, and seek a deeper understanding, fostering a culture of continuous learning and improvement.

- **Balanced Perspective:** Sound judgment is a critical quality for board members who are frequently confronted with pivotal decisions. The ability to weigh information, assess risks, and make informed decisions is paramount for steering the organization in the right direction.

- **Brave:** Board members must possess the courage to challenge the status quo, voice differing opinions, and expertly handle difficult decisions. Courageous leaders contribute to a robust governance framework by ensuring that critical issues are addressed, even when they involve uncomfortable conversations.

- **Maintain a Probing Attitude**: Professional skepticism is a discerning mindset that encourages board members to critically evaluate information and avoid complacency. Those who approach discussions with a healthy skepticism contribute to a culture of rigorous examination and risk mitigation.

- **Incisive - Get to the Core of Issues:** Incisiveness is a quality that enables board members to cut through complexity and identify the core issues at hand. This skill is invaluable for streamlining discussions, focusing on key priorities, and driving effective decision-making.

- **Analytical and Strategic:** Analytical and critical thinking are indispensable attributes for board members. The ability to analyze data, understand market trends, and develop strategic plans ensures that the board can proactively guide the organization toward sustainable growth.

- **Conflict Management Skills:** Given the diverse perspectives within a board, there is a greater need for effective conflict management skills. Board members should be adept at dealing with disagreements diplomatically, fostering collaboration, and ensuring that conflicts do not impede progress.

- **Communication Skills:** Strong communication skills are non-negotiable for board members. Whether conveying complex ideas, facilitating discussions, or articulating the organization's vision, effective communication is key to building consensus and driving alignment.

- **Good Listener and Relationship Builder:** Listen well, engage effectively, and build relationships and trust with fellow board members and executives. The ability to listen deeply and engage effectively is a key requirement for a NED. It helps to foster collaboration within the board and with the executive team. Building trust among peers and leadership is foundational for creating a healthy governance environment where different viewpoints can be aired and respected. For a NED, building strong relationships ensures smoother communication, encourages transparency, and enhances the effectiveness of board deliberations.

Thus, understanding and prioritizing these personal attributes empowers organizations to assemble a board that not only possesses the necessary expertise but also embodies the ethical principles and collaborative spirit essential for effective corporate governance.

4.1. Unlock The Power of Networking

The significance of your professional network cannot be overstated. Deliberate networking, both online and in-person, plays a pivotal role in positioning yourself for directorial roles. Here are key insights into leveraging your network for boardroom success:

- **Strategic Networking is Paramount:** Engage in proactive networking efforts, recognizing that connections are a cornerstone of board recruitment. Actively participate in industry events, conferences, and other forums to expand your network and increase your visibility.

- **Research Reveals Networking Patterns:** Studies consistently highlight that boards often rely on personal networks and word of mouth to identify potential candidates for directorial positions. As a NED or aspiring NED, you should understand this trend so you can strategically position yourself within networks that align with your board aspirations.

- **Forge Connections with Board Gatekeepers:** Identify and connect with individuals who serve as gatekeepers to the boardroom. These influencers may include current directors, executives, decision-makers or professionals with a direct link to board nomination processes. Cultivating relationships with these key figures enhances your chances of being considered for board opportunities.

- **Emphasize Quality over Quantity:** While a broad network is beneficial, prioritize quality connections over sheer quantity. Establish meaningful relationships with individuals who not only enhance your network's breadth but also bring depth through their industry expertise, influence, and credibility.

- **Position Yourself as a Valuable Resource:** Be intentional about showcasing your expertise and value within your network. Share insights, contribute to discussions, and position yourself as a thought leader in your industry. This positions you as a valuable resource, increasing the likelihood that others will recommend you for board positions.

- **Cultivate a Diverse Network:** Embrace diversity in your network, connecting with professionals from various industries, backgrounds, and experiences. A diverse network not only enriches your perspective but also increases the likelihood of being recommended for boards seeking a range of skills and perspectives.

- **Stay Informed and Relevant:** Keep abreast of industry trends, governance best practices, and emerging issues. Demonstrating a commitment to continuous learning and staying informed positions you as a forward-thinking and valuable candidate for board roles.

Your network is a dynamic asset in the pursuit of boardroom positions, which is why strategically nurturing connections, emphasizing quality relationships, and aligning with key influencers enhance your visibility and credibility.

4.2. Network Evaluation for Aspiring Board Members

Your network can bury your dream. In the journey towards securing a position on a corporate board, a deliberate and thorough review of your network and associations is indispensable. Consider the following comprehensive guide to optimizing your connections for success:

- **Behavioural and Social Review:** Conduct an introspective assessment of your behavior, habits, and friendships. Streamline your associates and align your lifestyle with the attributes befitting a corporate board member. Cultivate a professional demeanor that reflects the values and expectations of the boardroom.

- **Digital Footprint Management:** Scrutinize your digital presence, meticulously examining your social media profiles and connections. Eliminate or mitigate any content that may cast a negative shadow on your professional profile. Edit or delete posts, comments, and images that could compromise your reputation. Optimize your online persona by sharing relevant content that reinforces your desired image.

- **Building Meaningful Connections:** Intentionally connect with individuals who can contribute to your professional growth and boardroom aspirations. Join and actively participate in groups, both online and offline, that align with your industry and board interests. Strategic engagement with relevant communities, such as the Institute of Directors and professional clubs, can significantly enhance your visibility and network strength.

- **Dream-Supportive Network Construction:** Build a network that aligns with your dreams and aspirations. Actively engage in forums, associations, and groups that provide a supportive ecosystem for your professional goals. Consider affiliating with organizations like the Institute of Directors and clubs that offer valuable resources and networking opportunities conducive to your boardroom journey.

- **Intentional Time Investment:** Be discerning about how you invest your time and energy. Recognize the value of time as currency and allocate it purposefully. Surround yourself with individuals who inspire and contribute positively to your growth. Cultivate relationships that align with your vision and amplify your journey toward boardroom excellence.

- **Membership in Professional Forums:** Seek out and participate in forums and associations that cater to your industry and professional objectives. Active involvement in these platforms not only expands your knowledge base but also enhances your credibility among peers and potential board contacts.

As you join formal networking forums, you must become active and even get into leadership. In this way, you maximize your visibility.

The strategic curation of your network is a vital step towards boardroom success. Align your behaviors, refine your digital presence, and connect with the right individuals and forums to actively shape a network that supports and propels you toward your aspirations in the corporate governance arena.

4.3. Insights into the Dynamics of Your Professional Network

Discovering the different aspects of your network can profoundly impact your journey toward board career success. Consider these revelations and strategies for cultivating a robust professional network:

- **Network Multiplicity:** Your network extends beyond what may initially meet the eye. Understand this, and embrace the idea that you possess multiple networks, each with its unique potential and opportunities.

- **Endless Introductions:** Within your extensive network, there is invariably someone who can facilitate an introduction to another individual. Leverage this interconnected web by tapping into existing connections to open doors to new opportunities.

- **The Power of Preparation:** Conduct thorough homework and preparation when engaging with your network. Well-informed interactions not only demonstrate professionalism but also position you as someone worthy of valuable connections.

- **Targeted Networking:** Select specific targets within your network and craft precise requests. Define your objectives clearly and communicate them effectively to ensure that your networking efforts are purposeful and yield meaningful outcomes.

- **Reciprocity in Action:** Actively reciprocate when opportunities arise. Be attentive to the needs of your network and seize chances to contribute or offer assistance. Fostering a culture of reciprocity strengthens the bonds within your professional ecosystem.

- **Feedback Loop:** Acknowledge the advice or favors you receive by providing constructive feedback. This not only shows appreciation but also nurtures a culture of mutual growth and collaboration within your network.

- **Sustained Connectivity:** Maintain a proactive approach to staying connected. Regularly engage with your network, whether through professional platforms, events, or personal outreach. Sustained connectivity ensures that your network remains dynamic and responsive to your evolving needs.

4.4. What Are the Diverse Dimensions of Professional Connections?

As a NED, understanding the various types of connections is paramount for navigating the complexities of a board career success. Let's look at the roles and characteristics of different connection types:

- **Peers (*Collaborative Companions*):** Peers form a fundamental layer of your network, engaging in conversations and collaborations that foster idea generation and mutual growth.

This dynamic group encourages thinking aloud, posing innovative questions, and provides a grounding influence in the corporate journey.

- **Advisors (*Wisdom from Social and Professional Circles*):** Advisors contribute valuable insights and guidance, drawing from their experiences in both social and professional spheres. Their counsel serves as a compass, steering you through decision-making processes with wisdom acquired over time.

- **Mentors (*Guiding Lights in Personal and Professional Realms*):** Mentors play a pivotal role in offering guidance and support, drawing from their extensive experience in both personal and professional realms. They provide wisdom, share lessons, and act as trusted advisors on your journey toward corporate governance excellence.

- **Coaches (*Structured Guidance for Professional Growth*):** Distinct from mentors, coaches typically provide structured guidance and are often engaged on a paid basis. Their role is to facilitate skill development, performance enhancement, and goal achievement, ensuring a focused and results-driven approach.

- **Comrades (*Allies in Shared Struggles*):** Comrades are individuals who share common challenges and objectives. Together, you form a united front against shared obstacles, providing each other with support, encouragement, and shared understanding in the face of common battles. However, once the battle is over, do not be surprised if you drift apart.

- **Gatekeepers (*Custodians of Opportunities*):** Gatekeepers hold the keys to exclusive opportunities. Building relationships with these individuals opens doors to coveted board positions, valuable introductions, and unique prospects that can propel your governance aspirations.

- **Confidants** (*Trustworthy Partners in Confidentiality*): Confidants play a distinctive role in your network by being entrusted with confidential information. These individuals offer a safe space for sharing secrets, discussing sensitive matters, and seeking advice in a discreet and trustworthy environment.

- **Sponsors:** A sponsor is an influential and supportive individual who actively advocates for and promotes an individual's professional advancement. Unlike mentors who provide guidance and advice, sponsors go a step further by using their own credibility and influence to create opportunities, open doors, and endorse your career growth. A sponsor may help you by recommending you for key projects, promotions, or important assignments. Sponsors facilitate an individual's visibility, networking, and access to resources that can contribute to career progression.

4.5. Levels of Connections

Understanding and strategically maneuvering the various levels of professional connections is paramount for effective networking. These levels can be conceptualized as concentric circles, each representing a distinct sphere of influence and interaction.

1. **Inner Circle:** The inner circle comprises the closest and most intimate professional connections, often involving individuals with whom a Non-Executive Director (NED) shares a deep level of trust and collaboration. These connections may include fellow board members, top-level executives, and key stakeholders who play pivotal roles in decision-making processes. Building strong relationships within the inner circle is crucial for fostering a cohesive and unified governance approach. These connections offer a platform for open dialogue, critical alignment, and effective collaboration at the highest echelons of the organization.

2. **Middle Circle:** The middle circle expands beyond the inner sanctum to encompass a broader network of colleagues, industry peers, and professionals with whom the NED interacts regularly. These connections may involve fellow directors, executives from partner organizations, and industry experts. They contribute to a director's knowledge base and offer diverse perspectives on industry trends and best practices. The middle circle serves as a bridge between the innermost and outermost circles, facilitating the exchange of insights, information, and potential collaborative opportunities. Building a robust middle circle network enhances the director's ability to stay informed and adaptable in a dynamic business environment.

3. **Outer Circle:** The outer circle encompasses a broader sphere of connections, extending to individuals who may not have direct involvement in the day-to-day operations but still hold relevance to the director's overall professional setting. These connections could include professionals from related industries, regulatory bodies, and community leaders. While the interactions may be less frequent, they contribute to a holistic understanding of the external factors influencing the industry. The outer circle is vital for gaining a comprehensive perspective on industry trends, regulatory changes, and broader socioeconomic factors. Engaging with this circle allows NEDs to anticipate challenges and opportunities that may impact the organization in the long term.

The ability to distinguish these three levels and clearly and effectively manage and nurture relationships across the connections strategically is key for you to navigate the corporate governance space and position yourself for sustained success in your roles.

4.6. Types of Strategic Networks

Your professional growth and leadership development depends on your ability to harness the power of diverse networks. Here is a look into various types of networks that you can leverage to enhance your presence, build connections, and ascend into leadership roles.

- **Professional Bodies:** Professional bodies serve as essential networks for individuals in corporate governance. Active participation in professional bodies fosters industry-specific relationships, provides access to valuable resources, and enhances professional credibility. There are professional bodies for each industry, such as the Institute of Engineering and the Institute of Accountants. Find and join one or more relevant professional bodies within your industry, and your target industry.

- **Professional Networks:** Engaging with professional networks is a decisive move for you to thrive in corporate governance. These networks include esteemed organizations like Rotary Club, Toastmasters International, and Junior Chambers International. Participation in these platforms not only broadens your professional horizons but also hones leadership and communication skills.

- **Social and Charity Clubs:** Beyond the confines of strict professionalism, social and charity clubs play a significant role in networking. Associations with golf clubs, bowling leagues, yachting groups, and brand-specific clubs like the motor clubs create opportunities for informal interactions and relationship-building. These connections often extend and point you to the boardrooms, fostering a holistic sense of friendship and community.

- **Events and Conferences:** Actively engaging with events and conferences is a dynamic strategy for networking in corporate governance. Attendance at industry-specific conferences and events provides a platform for you to showcase your expertise, exchange ideas with industry leaders, and establish yourself as an influential figure.

4.7. Strategies for Effective Networking

Dealing with the intricate corporate governance environment requires more than just technical expertise; it demands a keen understanding of the power of networks. By strategically engaging with professional bodies, diverse networks, social clubs, and events, you can carve a path toward leadership roles, contributing significantly to the dynamic world of corporate governance. Here are some of the tactics one can apply:

- **Strategic Engagement:** Merely being a part of a network is insufficient; strategic engagement is key. You should actively participate in network activities, contribute to discussions, and seek leadership roles within these networks to maximize your influence.

- **Building a Personal Brand:** Developing a personal brand within these networks will help you stand out. This involves showcasing unique skills, sharing insights, and positioning oneself as a thought leader within the corporate governance space.

- **Diversity in Networks:** To create a robust network, you should diversify your engagements. Balancing involvement in professional bodies, professional networks, and social clubs provides a well-rounded approach to networking that goes beyond industry boundaries.

- **Continuous Learning:** Networking is not just about making connections; it's also about staying updated with industry trends. Attending workshops, seminars, and continuous learning opportunities within networks ensures that you remain relevant and informed.

- **Mentorship and Sponsorship:** Actively seeking mentorship and sponsorship within networks can propel your career in corporate governance. Establishing relationships with seasoned professionals fosters personal and professional growth, opening doors to leadership opportunities.

4.8. The Enduring Allure of Golf in Business Culture

The game of golf has long held a prominent place in the lives of business professionals, transcending its origins as a leisure activity. In this section, we look at the multifaceted reasons why many businesspeople, irrespective of their industry, find themselves drawn to the golf course. From its inclusive nature to its unique position in the corporate world, golf serves as more than just a sport; it's a dynamic arena for professional networking and personal development.

- **Sport for Every Professional:** Golf's appeal lies in its accessibility to professionals across industries. Unlike some sports that demand specific physical attributes or intense training, golf welcomes individuals of varying fitness levels and ages. This inclusivity makes it an ideal choice for businesspeople seeking a sport that accommodates diverse skill sets.

- **Cross-Industry Participation:** Beyond the corporate realm, golf attracts individuals from diverse backgrounds, including other sports professionals. The golf course serves as a common ground where individuals from different industries can come together, fostering cross-industry connections and collaborations.

- **Business Networking:** Golf has become synonymous with business networking. The golf course provides a unique setting for informal discussions and relationship-building. Many deals have been struck, and partnerships formed over a round of golf, making it an integral part of corporate culture.

- **Potential Professional Golfer:** Golf offers a rare opportunity for business professionals to aspire to become professional golfers themselves. While not everyone may reach the pinnacle of the sport, the pursuit of excellence on the golf course mirrors the dedication and discipline required in the business world.

- **Unlikely Participants:** Interestingly, even individuals with less-than-savory backgrounds, including some with criminal ties, find themselves drawn to golf. The sport's inclusive environment provides a neutral space where diverse individuals can interact, transcending societal stereotypes.

- **Lifelong Engagement:** Golf is one of the few sports that you can play throughout your entire life. From a young age to retirement, the golf course accommodates players at every stage of life. This longevity adds to the sport's appeal for business professionals looking for a consistent and enduring recreational activity.

4.9. The Benefits of Playing Golf

The role of golf becomes apparent not just as a sport but as a vital aspect of professional life. From its inclusive nature to its unique position as a platform for business networking, golf continues to be a common thread that ties together professionals from various industries, contributing to the tapestry of corporate culture.

- **Relaxed Environment for Discussions:** The relaxed atmosphere of a golf course creates an environment conducive to open discussions. Businesspeople often find that the informal setting fosters genuine conversations, allowing you to connect on a more personal level.

- **Strategic Business Meetings:** Golf is frequently utilized as a strategic setting for business meetings. The collaborative nature of the game encourages teamwork, providing a unique perspective on an individual's interpersonal and problem-solving skills.

- **Health and Wellness:** Beyond the professional advantages, golf promotes health and wellness. The physical activity involved in playing golf contributes to overall well-being, aligning with the growing emphasis on a healthy work-life balance in corporate culture.

4.10. Cautionary Networking Considerations

While networking is an indispensable tool in the corporate governance toolbox, it's crucial to approach it with a mindful and strategic mindset. Given this, what are the set of cautious considerations that you should keep in mind as you engage in professional networking? From managing expectations to handling online connections, this guide provides insights into creating meaningful connections while avoiding potential pitfalls.

- **Decisive Networking:** When venturing into the realm of networking, you must connect with people without expecting immediate benefits. Develop a plan that aligns with your professional goals and ensures that your interactions are purposeful and meaningful.

- **Inclusivity in Connections:** Effective networking involves connecting with individuals of varying influence, from high-profile executives to emerging professionals. Avoid restricting your connections to only those at the top, as meaningful relationships can often be cultivated at all levels of an organization or industry.

- **Online Etiquette:** In the digital age, online networking is a prominent aspect of professional connections. If a connection online becomes bothersome or unproductive, do not hesitate to utilize functions like blocking, unfollowing, or even reporting a connection or profile. Maintaining a positive and focused online presence is crucial for your professional image.

- **Managing Physical Connections:** While face-to-face connections offer unique opportunities, it's important to navigate them cautiously. Avoid misunderstandings, especially in the context of romantic relationships or false expectations. Maintaining professionalism in physical connections ensures that networking efforts remain focused on career growth.

- **Graceful Acceptance of Rejection:** Rejection is an inevitable part of networking. Whether it's a declined connection request or a failed collaboration. Accepting rejection gracefully ensures no damage to your professional image. Use it as an opportunity for learning and improvement rather than allowing it to hinder your future networking endeavors.

- **Networking for Introverts:** Networking is not exclusive to extroverts; even introverts can excel in this domain. For those who may find social interactions challenging, studying materials on networking as an introvert can provide valuable insights and strategies for effective networking without compromising your comfort zone.

- **Setting Clear Objectives:** Before embarking on a networking journey, define clear objectives. Whether it's expanding professional connections, seeking mentorship, or exploring collaborative opportunities, having a well-defined plan guides your networking efforts and ensures that they align with your career goals.

- **Regularly Assessing Connections:** Periodically assess your network to ensure that it remains aligned with your professional objectives. Prune connections that no longer contribute to your growth, and actively seek new connections that align with your evolving goals.

- **Building Genuine Relationships:** Successful networking is not just about the number of connections but the quality of relationships. Focus on building genuine connections by actively engaging in meaningful conversations, sharing insights, and offering support to others in your network.

The concept of personal branding has evolved into a powerful tool for professionals. This section explores the essence of personal branding, a dynamic and compelling public image that can significantly influence success in the corporate world. Drawing inspiration from "*The Brand Called You*" by Peter Montoya and Tim Vandehey, let's look at the components of personal branding and the transformative potential of refining your existing brand. We will start from the beginning.

- **Definition of Personal Brand:** A personal brand is not just a logo or a tagline; it is a comprehensive and powerful public image that reflects your values, expertise, and unique qualities. It's the narrative that distinguishes you in the professional sphere, shaping how others perceive and remember you.

- **Dynamic Nature of Personal Branding**: Recognizing that you already possess a brand, the journey of personal branding involves refining and evolving it over time. Whether you are initiating a change in your career, aiming for a leadership role, or seeking to enhance your professional impact, the process of personal branding is an ongoing and dynamic endeavor.

5.1. The Impact of Personal Presence on Professional Perception

The significance of personal presence cannot be overstated. Let's look at how various elements of your appearance contribute to how seriously you are taken in a professional context. From physical attributes to cultural considerations, understanding and managing your personal presence is crucial for cultivating a positive and impactful professional image.

- **Physical Appearance:** Your physical appearance is often the first impression you make on others. Consider elements such as hairstyle, body size, and overall grooming. While there is no one-size-fits-all standard, presenting yourself in a polished and well-maintained manner communicates a level of professionalism that influences how seriously others perceive you.

- **Dressing for Impact:** The way you dress is a powerful aspect of personal presence. Dressing appropriately for the occasion and being intentional about your wardrobe choices can convey a sense of competence and reliability. Understanding the dress code within your industry and adapting your attire accordingly demonstrates a keen awareness of professional norms.

- **Posture and Body Language:** Your posture speaks volumes about your confidence and professionalism. Whether standing, walking, or greeting others, maintaining good posture exudes self-assuredness. Non-verbal cues, such as a firm handshake and confident body language, contribute significantly to how seriously you are taken in a professional setting.

- **Voice and Communication:** The way you speak is a key element of personal presence. Pay attention to your tone, projection, accent, and overall confidence in your communication. Record yourself speaking and listen to how you sound. In this way, you will know how to adjust your voice. A well-modulated and articulate voice commands attention and enhances your ability to convey ideas effectively.

- **Cultural Considerations:** Cultural differences play a vital role in personal presence. Understanding and respecting cultural differences is crucial, especially in a globalized corporate environment. For example, factors that bring us diversity can influence how we are perceived, and being culturally sensitive contributes to positive professional interactions.

5.2. Understanding Yourself

Your personal presence is a dynamic force that shapes perceptions. By conscientiously managing aspects such as physical appearance, dressing for impact, maintaining a confident posture, refining communication skills, and understanding cultural influences, you can cultivate a personal presence that commands respect and contributes to your success in the professional arena. All this comes from your self-awareness assessment.

Note: We discussed Self-awareness and Personal Strategy in Chapter 2. Revisiting the chapter is advisable.

- **Introversion and Extroversion:** You should strive to understand your personality type, whether you are introverted or extroverted. Introverts may excel in one-on-one interactions, while extroverts thrive in group settings. Tailoring your approach to align with your natural tendencies ensures that your personal presence is authentic and comfortable.

- **Energy Levels:** Recognizing your energy levels is key to managing your personal presence. Whether you draw energy from social interactions or require moments of solitude to recharge, being mindful of your energy dynamics enables you to navigate professional situations effectively without compromising your well-being.

- **Perception Management:** Consider how others perceive you. Solicit feedback, assess your strengths and weaknesses, and work on areas that may impact your professional image. Developing self-awareness allows you to project a consistent and positive personal presence.

5.3. Branding Considerations

Strategic branding is a fundamental aspect that can significantly impact professional success. This section explores key considerations in crafting a powerful personal brand that resonates at the corporate governance level. From physical appearance to competencies and differentiators, we investigate the components that contribute to a compelling professional identity.

- **Physical Appearance:** Your physical appearance is a visible representation of your personal brand. Consider what you want people to perceive from the outside. Evaluate whether your clothing, hairstyle, and grooming align with your authentic self and convey the professional image you wish to project.

- **Personality and Behaviour:** How you interact, speak, and relate to others plays a pivotal 1 role in your personal brand. Assess whether your personality and behavior reflect your best self. Authentic interactions contribute to a positive brand image, fostering trust and credibility in the corporate governance arena.

- **Competencies:** Identifying and showcasing your competencies, skills, and talents is integral to personal branding. Clearly define your strengths and recognize what you excel at. This self-awareness forms the foundation for communicating your value proposition.

- **Differentiations:** Consider what sets you apart from others in your professional sphere. Reflect on what you have consistently been recognized for and the skills that people tend to notice in your work. Recognizing your differentiators allows you to emphasize your unique contributions within the corporate governance framework.

- **Presentation Platforms:** Knowing where and how to present your personal brand is crucial. Utilize platforms such as your biography, professional resume, and networking within professional organizations to strategically showcase your brand. Engaging in volunteer efforts, participating in public speaking events, and maintaining a strong presence on social media are additional avenues for elevating your personal brand.

- **Consistency Across Platforms:** Ensure consistency in your branding across various platforms. Whether it's your professional resume, social media profiles, or public speaking engagements, maintaining a cohesive brand message reinforces your professional identity.

- **Leveraging Professional Organizations:** Active participation in professional organizations within the corporate governance realm provides a strategic platform for presenting your personal brand. Networking within these organizations allows you to connect with industry professionals and establish yourself as a recognized figure.

- **Volunteer Efforts:** Engaging in volunteer efforts aligned with your professional values not only contributes to societal well-being but also enhances your personal brand. Volunteer work showcases your commitment to making a positive impact beyond your professional responsibilities.

- **Public Speaking Opportunities:** Public speaking events present a powerful platform for communicating your expertise and personal brand. Whether participating in conferences, seminars, or workshops, sharing your insights enhances your visibility and establishes you as a thought leader within the corporate governance space.

- **Intentional Use of Social Media:** Maintain an active and professional presence on social media platforms. Utilize these channels to share industry insights, network with professionals, and showcase your achievements. Social media serves as a dynamic tool for building and reinforcing your personal brand.

5.4. More Ways to Enhance Your Professional Image

A polished and professional image is a valuable asset. In this section, we discuss an array of strategies to enhance your personal image, transcending beyond traditional approaches. From grooming to potential relocations, these comprehensive strategies aim to empower you to present your best selves.

1) **Grooming:** Grooming is a foundational aspect of personal image. Regular grooming practices, including well-maintained hair, facial care, and appropriate attire, contribute to a polished and professional appearance. Consistency in grooming reflects your commitment to presenting yourself at your best.

2) **Dental Work:** Dental aesthetics play a significant role in your overall image. Consider dental work to address issues such as alignment, discoloration, or other dental concerns. A bright and confident smile enhances your professional presence, leaving a lasting positive impression.

3) **Eye/Sight Correction:** Clear and confident vision is essential in professional settings. Addressing vision concerns through corrective measures, such as eyeglasses or contact lenses, not only improves your visual acuity but also contributes to an overall well-groomed appearance.

4) **Skin Work:** Addressing skin concerns and blemishes enhances your complexion and contributes to a healthier and more radiant appearance, bolstering your professional image. This may include

reducing or removing certain visible tattoos. Tattoos are often associated with gangsterism and the prison.

5) **Speech Therapy:** Effective communication is a cornerstone of professional success. Consider speech therapy to refine your accent and public speaking skills. Clear and articulate communication not only fosters better understanding but also boosts confidence in professional interactions.

6) **Name Change:** For some individuals, a name change can be a vital move to align with their professional aspirations. Whether it's adopting a more distinctive name or addressing personal preferences, a well-considered name change can contribute to a renewed and intentional personal image.

7) **Relocation:** Geographic relocation can be a transformative strategy for business or personal improvement. Each city has areas that are considered to be affluent or prominent. Brands of residents of these areas enjoy being associated with the name of the area. Moving to a different part of the city, to another, or even another country not only offers a fresh start and new opportunities but becomes part of your brand. A change in environment can influence both personal and professional growth.

Conduct a comprehensive self-assessment to identify areas for improvement in your personal image. When considering a name change or relocation, be mindful of cultural sensitivities. Ensure that these decisions align with your personal and professional identity while respecting the cultural contexts in which you operate. Personal improvement is a journey that requires dedication and a long-term commitment. Incorporate these strategies into your lifestyle and routine, ensuring that they become integral aspects of your ongoing personal development.

5.5. Building a Robust Professional Brand

In this section, we briefly discuss strategies you can implement to optimize your online presence and construct a cohesive and impactful professional brand that resonates within the corporate governance arena.

- **LinkedIn Profile Excellence:** To establish a compelling professional brand, begin with optimizing your LinkedIn profile. This involves more than just completing the basic sections. Dive deep into detailing your experience and qualifications, providing a distinctive narrative of your professional journey. The summary section of your profile should quickly capture the viewers' attention by expertly articulating your skills and experience in a few sentences.

  Place emphasis on pertinent skills and spotlight experiences that align with your career goals. An engaging and well-optimized LinkedIn profile serves as a dynamic gateway for professional networking and opportunities. This is so valuable that some professionals hire professional LinkedIn profile writers and designers to make sure they spruce up their profiles for maximum impact.

- **Impactful Personal Website:** Creating a distinctive personal website serves as a virtual showcase of your expertise, too. You must design this platform to meticulously reflect your unique personal brand. Feature not only your professional achievements but also showcase noteworthy projects and activities. Utilize multimedia elements such as videos and images to create a visually engaging narrative that resonates with your audience. A well-crafted personal website is a powerful tool to leave a lasting impression on stakeholders and potential collaborators.

- **Diversifying Online Presence:** Extend the reach of your professional brand by expanding your presence across various online platforms. Consider platforms beyond LinkedIn and your personal website to ensure a comprehensive and impactful representation. Each platform can serve a distinct purpose, from engaging in industry-specific conversations on forums to sharing insights on professional platforms. This diversified approach enhances your visibility and positions you as a thought leader in your field.

- **Craft a Compelling Board CV/Resume:** Document your professional journey meticulously through a board CV/Resume. This document should provide more than a chronological list of roles; it should encapsulate your achievements, skills, and the impact you've made throughout your career. Tailor it to highlight your qualifications and professional development. A well-crafted board CV/resume is a foundational piece that complements your online presence, offering a detailed overview for those seeking a deeper understanding of your capabilities and contributions. In the next chapter, we will discuss in detail how to create a board CV.

- **Virtual Meeting Platforms:** When attending virtual meetings or webinars, use your real name and add a profile photo to ensure you are easily recognizable. Make sure to contribute by speaking up or sharing a comment in the chat before leaving. This boosts your visibility and can spark curiosity among other participants, prompting them to look you up online and potentially connect with you. In some webinars, participants are even encouraged to share their LinkedIn profiles in the chat, making it easier to network.

- **Personal Email Signature:** While many have a signature for their work emails, consider creating one for your personal email, too. It reflects professionalism in all aspects of your communication. Use this signature to highlight your skills and expertise, leaving a lasting impression even in personal exchanges.

5.6. Desire, Competency, and Market Reality

An alignment of these three critical factors – your desired board position, your competency, and available positions in the market – can lead to the optimal scenario. This convergence occurs when your dream Non-Executive Director (NED) role, your unique set of skills, experience, and competence, and the existing landscape of NED positions in the job market intersect harmoniously.

Let's explore each dimension further:

- **Aspirations and Desired NED Role:** You have your vision for the ideal NED position. You may also have the industry, organization size, and specific responsibilities that resonate with your professional aspirations.

- **Skills, Experience, and Professional Competence:** You possess a spectrum of skills, experiences, and competencies you bring to the table as a NED. You may be proficient in areas such as financial acumen, risk management, industry knowledge, and stakeholder engagement.

- **NED Positions Available in the Market:** These are positions currently in the NED job market.

Clearly understand your governance, strategic oversight, and leadership dynamics, envisioning a role that not only aligns with your career goals but also fulfills your broader sense of purpose and contribution. Recognize the unique value you offer to boards and how your expertise can contribute to effective governance and key decision-making. Research on the opportunities in various sectors, considering the diversity of organizations, their governance structures, and the evolving expectations for board members. Stay informed about industry trends, regulatory changes, and emerging priorities that influence the demand for NEDs.

This market intelligence will empower you to position yourself strategically.

6.1. Why Do You Need A Well-Crafted Board CV?

A board CV (Curriculum Vitae), interchangeably referred to as a board resume or director's resume, serves as a pivotal tool in building a board career. It is meticulously crafted and designed to highlight your qualifications and your experience, presenting a comprehensive overview of your professional journey. More than a mere record of accomplishments, a well-constructed board CV strategically showcases an individual's unique attributes and suitability for a board position. The creation of a compelling and distinctive board CV becomes paramount, as it not only reflects the individual's expertise but also sets you apart as a standout candidate in the eyes of discerning decision-makers.

6.2. Key Differences Between a Board CV and a Standard CV

A board CV is different from a normal CV in several ways. Here are some of the ways it is different from a Normal CV.

- **Purpose:** The primary purpose of a Board CV is to showcase an individual's qualifications, expertise, and experience to secure a position on corporate boards, advisory committees, or sub-committees. It emphasizes leadership, governance knowledge, strategy, risk, and corporate governance abilities, as well as the potential to add value to the organization's decision-making processes at the governance level.

- **Audience:** The target audience for a Board CV includes board nominating committees, corporate governance specialists, company secretaries, and other board members. It aims to appeal to these individuals responsible for selecting qualified candidates for board positions.

- **Content Emphasis:** A Board CV highlights executive-level leadership experience, corporate governance expertise, strategic planning skills, and other relevant board-related qualifications. It may also emphasize a candidate's contributions to prior boards, committee memberships, and governance-related accomplishments. It focuses on highlighting skills, knowledge, competencies, and experience with executive committees, boards, policies, and oversight.

- **Length and Format:** A Board CV is typically shorter, ranging from one to two pages. It is concise and tailored to highlight specific corporate governance skills and experiences directly related to the candidate's leadership abilities, governance experience, and relevant achievements.

- **Focus on Governance:** A Board CV places significant emphasis on governance awareness, adherence to ethical standards, risk, strategy, and understanding of board-level responsibilities. It may also highlight the candidate's contribution to ESG issues, as ESG issues are increasingly valued on boards. Highlight your experience with reporting to boards, engaging with boards, and engaging with executive committees.

- **Tailoring:** Board CVs are often customized for specific board positions. You may tailor your CVs to align with the specific requirements and expectations of the board that you are applying to.

6.3. Crafting a Compelling Non-Executive Director CV

In the pursuit of a Non-Executive Director (NED) role, the creation of a persuasive and refined board CV is crucial. Here's an expanded guide covering key elements or sections to ensure your CV stands out:

- **Length Consideration:** Strive for conciseness in your board CV, aiming for a length of no more than two pages. However, acknowledge that certain situations may demand a more detailed account of your qualifications, experience, and achievements.

- **Should You Include a Photo?:** While including a photograph is common, exercise caution as it may inadvertently lead to discrimination. Weigh the potential benefits against the risks, considering the norms of the industry and the specific context of the board positions you are pursuing. For example, not all printers are similar – in some cases, your printed photo may not look as presentable as it is in the digital format.

- **Board Profile (One-Paragraph Board Pitch):** Begin your CV with a powerful one-paragraph board pitch to enhance your board profile. This succinctly introduces your unique value proposition, setting the tone for what follows and capturing the attention of decision-makers.

- **Value Proposition (Showcasing Expertise and Success):** In this section, articulate your value proposition by emphasizing your governance experience. Highlight both non-executive and executive board and committee roles, showcasing your expertise in specialized areas such as Strategy, Ethics, Risk, and ESG (Environmental, Social, and Governance). Illuminate your executive successes and career highlights to demonstrate your impact and effectiveness.

- **Qualifications & Certifications (Building Credibility):** Next, you strengthen your credibility by detailing your qualifications and certifications. Include professional registrations and illustrate your commitment to ongoing professional development, underscoring your dedication to staying abreast of industry trends and best practices.

- **Extra-Professional Activities & Interests (Holistic Professionalism):** Broaden the scope of your professional profile by incorporating extra-professional activities and interests. Highlight memberships in relevant professional bodies, showcase any awards received, and emphasize the robust networks you have cultivated within your industry.

- **Credible Referees (Establishing Trust):** Conclude your CV by providing credible referees, available upon request. This serves as a testament to your professional standing and offers an avenue for prospective employers to verify and validate your qualifications and suitability for NED roles.

In summary, meticulously addressing the above components catapults your NED CV into a dynamic tool that not only outlines your qualifications but also strategically communicates your unique value proposition. Annexure One contains templates for Non-Executive Director (NED) resumes/CVs that you may find useful.

7.1. Compiling Your Career Narrative

Your career or professional story is a powerful tool in positioning yourself for NED roles. Strive to skilfully narrate your career story to not only provide a comprehensive overview of your professional journey but also establish a compelling case for your candidacy. Narrate your career story during networking events and in interviews. This is your story. Master it and keep improving it. Make your story impactful and memorable so that you stand out. Here's an expanded guide on how to tell your story effectively:

- ❏ **Self-Assessment and Profile Understanding:** Begin by thoroughly assessing yourself and your career history. Identify your advantages and disadvantages, acknowledging areas of strength and areas for growth. Leverage these insights to shape your narrative, emphasizing how your unique profile positions you as a valuable asset for boards. Refer to Chapter Two, where we covered 'Self-Awareness and Personal Strategy,' Use the results of the assessments.

- ❏ **Recognizing Board Attractiveness:** Understand what makes you attractive to boards. Highlight capabilities, skills, and experiences that align with the expectations of NED roles. Showcase your strategy skills, governance expertise, and any industry-specific knowledge that sets you apart.

- ❏ **Customizing for Board Service:** As you tell your story, tailor your approach for various board service opportunities. Whether in interviews or networking, tell your story thoughtfully and authentically. Emphasize logical career choices with clear explanations, utilizing a simple and chronological format.

Demonstrate how your skills and experiences align with the specific needs of the board.

- ❑ **Storytelling Excellence:** Present your career story as a compelling narrative. Highlight logical transitions in your professional journey, ensuring a clear and understandable chronological format. Emphasise positions where you made a significant impact, emphasizing measurable accomplishments and promotions. Remember, a promotion is an outstanding achievement. Only a few people get promoted. Most people rise in their careers by changing jobs.

- ❑ **Measurable Accomplishments and Promotions:** Make it easy for your audience to identify your successes. Clearly articulate your goals and accomplishments, emphasizing measurable outcomes. This clarity adds weight to your narrative, showcasing your ability to set and achieve objectives.

- ❑ **Credible Transitions and Moves:** Establish a clear and credible pathway to the NED roles you seek. Showcase your career transitions as strategic moves that align with your overarching goals. Demonstrate a thoughtful progression that positions you as the ideal candidate for board service.

- ❑ **Accuracy and Recognized References:** Ensure accuracy in presenting facts and dates. Avoid misrepresentations or vague claims that could undermine your credibility. Highlight recognized mentors and references, further validating your achievements and suitability for NED positions.

- ❑ **Alignment with Board Objectives:** Do not forget to indicate your ability and desire to fulfill what boards are seeking. Illustrate how your skills, experiences, and career choices align with the expectations of non-executive directorship, showcasing your readiness to contribute meaningfully.

In simple terms, your story is an outcome of your career strategy. In your story, show that all your career moves are part of your career strategy. Some of your career moves may not be according to your plan or even due to unfortunate events. However, find the good and opportunities from them. Most often, these unfortunate turns and detours contribute useful skills to the career.

7.2. Crafting an Impactful Cover Letter

A cover letter is also called a letter of motivation. Its purpose is to introduce yourself, convince why they should hire you, and, if necessary, address any concerns the hiring manager might have with your profile.

In composing a compelling cover letter for a Non-Executive Director (NED) position, it's essential to go beyond the basics and weave a narrative that resonates with the board.

Here's an expanded guide on key elements or sections to include:

- **Passion for the Role:** Express genuine enthusiasm for the NED role you are applying for. Elaborate on why this specific position aligns with your professional aspirations and how your skills and experiences uniquely position you to contribute meaningfully.

- **Your Profile (A Distinctive Introduction):** Provide a succinct yet comprehensive overview of your professional profile. Highlight key accomplishments, experiences, and expertise that directly correlate with the expectations and requirements of a NED. Craft this section as a snapshot that leaves a lasting impression.

- **Addressing Concerns:** Proactively address any potential concerns that might arise in your candidacy. Be transparent and strategic in explaining how your skills and experiences compensate for any perceived shortcomings, turning potential concerns into opportunities for growth and learning.

- **Something Memorable (Stand Out from the Crowd):** Introduce an element that makes your application memorable. This could be a unique professional achievement, a distinctive skill set, or a personal anecdote that illustrates your approach to governance. Engage the reader's attention and ensure that your cover letter stands out in a competitive field.

- **Passion for the Organisation:** Demonstrate not only your passion for the role but also your enthusiasm for the organization or organization you are seeking to join. Showcase your understanding of the organization's mission, values, and strategic goals. Align your aspirations with its vision to convey a genuine commitment to its success.

- **Ability to Address Current Challenges:** Research and reiterate your ability and commitment to addressing any current challenges that the organization may have. Showcase your proactive mindset, emphasizing your willingness to collaborate and contribute effectively to overcome challenges and drive positive outcomes.

- **Closing with Confidence:** Conclude your cover letter with a confident closing statement. Reiterate your passion for the role and express your eagerness for the opportunity to contribute to the organization's success. Provide your contact information and express your readiness for further discussion.

7.3. Setting Up for a Successful Interview

Combining a powerful board pitch, authentic passion, and cultural acumen positions you as a candidate who not only understands the business dynamics but also contributes positively to the overall board culture and objectives. Here are some key insights and strategies to be mindful of for a successful interview:

- ❑ **Craft an Impactful Board Pitch:** Begin with a compelling board pitch that showcases your skills, such as risk management, strategic direction, governance, and avenues for growth or influence. Showcase your unique perspective, experiences, and expertise to demonstrate your value to the board. Your board pitch is unique to you. Write your board pitch, start using it, and continuously refine it to ensure it sets you apart.

- ❑ **Cohesive Personal Branding:** Ensure a seamless alignment between your LinkedIn profile, CV, your personal story, and your board pitch. Consistency across these platforms strengthens your professional brand and presents a unified narrative to potential boards. This harmonized approach reinforces your credibility and showcases a well-thought-out professional identity.

- ❑ **Communicate Your Passion Effectively:** Articulate your passion in three critical dimensions: for the role, the organization, and its products or services. Provide tangible proof of your enthusiasm through specific examples or experiences that illustrate your commitment. Whether it's your engagement with the organization's mission, your belief in the industry's potential, or your excitement about the products/services offered, convey your passion authentically.

- ❑ **Decode the Industry and Organisation Culture:** Recognize the significance of understanding the specific code of conduct within the industry or organization you are aspiring to join as a NED. Pay attention to simple things such as dress code, cultural expectations, and language preferences, whether technical or otherwise. This cultural awareness enhances your ability to integrate seamlessly into the organizational fabric, fostering positive relationships with board members and stakeholders.

- ❑ **Dress Code Etiquette:** Appreciate the importance of adhering to the dress code appropriate for board meetings and related events. Align your attire with the cultural norms of the boardroom, reflecting professionalism and respect for the established standards.

- ❑ **Cultural Experience Sensitivity:** Acknowledge the diversity of cultural experiences within the business or industry. Develop a keen sensitivity to different cultural backgrounds and perspectives, fostering inclusivity and effective collaboration.

- ❑ **Language Mastery:** Understand the technical and non-technical language types prevalent in the industry or organization. Effective communication is paramount in boardrooms; thus, mastering the language specific to your sector ensures that you contribute meaningfully to discussions and decision-making processes.

- ❑ **Thorough Homework:** Approach each stage of the directorship journey with meticulous preparation:

  - *At Application:* Understand the specific requirements of the position and tailor your application accordingly. Highlight the skills and experiences that directly align with the board's expectations.
  - *Pre-Interview Planning:* Research the organization extensively. Familiarize yourself with its values, mission, and recent developments. Anticipate potential questions and prepare thoughtful responses that demonstrate your understanding of the board's needs.
  - *At the Interview:* Showcase your preparedness by providing well-informed responses. Engage in discussions that reflect your knowledge of the organization's challenges and opportunities. Demonstrate how your expertise aligns with the board's strategic objectives.

- *Post-Interview:* Reflect on the interview experience. Identify areas of improvement and, if applicable, send a follow-up message expressing gratitude for the opportunity and reiterating your interest in the role.
- *Pre-Appointment Due Diligence:* Before accepting a NED appointment, conduct thorough due diligence on the organization. Understand its financial health, governance structure, and potential challenges. This proactive approach ensures that you align with the values and objectives of the board.

Now, let's look at these issues in detail.

7.4. Board Interview Preparation

By addressing the following key points in your board interview preparation, you not only position yourself as a knowledgeable and strategic candidate but also demonstrate your dedication to contributing meaningfully to the organization as a NED.

- **In-Depth Organisation and Industry Research:** Thoroughly research the organisation, understanding its offerings, client base, and market footprint. Equip yourself to respond to questions with insightful comments that reflect your comprehensive knowledge of the organization and its industry context.

- **Strategic Understanding of Opportunities and Challenges:** Study the critical landscape by identifying the opportunities and challenges facing the organization. Understand whether the organization is undergoing transformative changes or experiencing high growth through acquisitions. Formulate your responses to articulate how your unique skill set and experience will contribute to addressing these strategic aspects, demonstrating your value-add to the board.

- **Familiarize Yourself with Board Members:** Prior to the interview, gather information about the board members you will be meeting. Understand your backgrounds, experiences, and skill sets. This knowledge enables you to tailor your responses and engage in informed discussions during the interview.

- **Emphasize Your Value Proposition:** Craft a compelling narrative that highlights the specific value you will bring to the board. Clearly articulate what sets you apart and how your expertise complements the existing board composition. Showcase your unique perspectives and contributions that others may not offer.

- **Evaluate Time Commitment:** Assess the time commitment required, considering the number of board, pre-board, and committee meetings. Demonstrate your capacity to fulfill these commitments effectively while maintaining a balance with your other professional responsibilities.

- **Understand the Board Compensation Structure:** Review the organization's annual proxy circular to understand the structure of board compensation. Familiarize yourself with the frequency of board compensation reviews. This knowledge positions you to discuss compensation matters confidently during the interview.

- **Address Potential Conflicts of Interest:** Reflect on any potential conflicts of interest that may arise in the role. Prepare to address these proactively, showcasing your ability to navigate and mitigate conflicts while maintaining a focus on the organization's best interests.

- **Advocate for Diversity:** Articulate how your appointment would enhance the board's composition, considering factors such as gender, location, age, and other relevant demographics. Support your points with statistics from reputable surveys, reinforcing the importance of diversity in effective governance.

- **Conduct Due Diligence Before and After the Interview:** Prior to the interview, conduct thorough due diligence about the organization. After the interview, continue to gather insights to deepen your understanding. This ongoing diligence showcases your commitment to being well-informed and engaged throughout the selection process.

During an interview, it is essential to ask relevant questions that demonstrate your interest in the role, highlight your competency, and foster a connection with the interview panel. Shift the tone of the interview from a formal interrogation to an engaging conversation. Never leave the interview without asking insightful questions. Be well-prepared by familiarizing yourself with common interview questions for board positions, as well as the key questions you should ask, which are provided in Annexure Two.

7.5. How To Deal With Rejections After the Interview

Here are some reasons why you may not have been appointed for the board position:

- **Stronger Competition:** Other candidates may have had a more compelling overall profile. This could include more relevant experience, higher qualifications, stronger interview performance, better leadership or communication skills, realistic compensation expectations, shorter notice periods, greater enthusiasm for the role, stronger rapport with the interviewers, more favorable references, or even internal candidates also being considered. These are valid and genuine reasons.
- **Not the Right Fit for the Role:** There may have been a mismatch in skills, where the selected candidate possessed expertise or experience more closely aligned with the specific requirements of the

position. Alternatively, the decision may have been based on cultural fit, with the company believing another candidate would better complement the organization's culture or team dynamics. These are also reasonable factors.

- **Faulty Decision-Making:** In some cases, the interview panel may not have a clear understanding of the kind of candidate they truly need. As a result, they might appoint someone who is not the right choice, only to realize it later. Sometimes, they may not even recognize that the person selected does not provide the value the organization actually requires. If this is the reason you were not appointed, perhaps you should be relieved.

In case of rejection, embrace it as a stepping stone to improvement. Seeking feedback proactively, turning setbacks into opportunities, and leveraging relationships are some of the things that help you resiliently deal with rejection and pave the way for future success in the dynamic world of board appointments.

Here are some key points to be aware of:

1. **Anticipate and Prepare for Rejection:** Rejection is a common aspect of the NED application process. Even seasoned board directors may face rejection, which can be disheartening, particularly when possessing the requisite qualifications. Instead of succumbing to discouragement, view rejection as an opportunity for growth and learning. Reflect on the experience, analyze shortcomings, and consider avenues for improvement. Transform rejection into resilience by asking:

   - What lessons can I learn from this process?
   - What adjustments do I need to make in order to leverage future opportunities?
   - How can I enhance future performance?
   - How can I expand my network to connect with individuals who can provide guidance or referrals?

- What feedback can I seek from others to gain a better understanding of where I can improve?
- What specific skills or knowledge should I develop further to increase my competitiveness for future opportunities?

2. **Seek Constructive Feedback:** Actively seek feedback at every stage of the process. If you do not make it to the interview shortlist, you can inquire about the shortcomings in your application from recruiters or selection panels. Consider engaging a mentor for an independent perspective on your board pitch, resume, and long-term aspirations. For those who reached the interview stage, seek candid feedback on your performance. Understand what set successful candidates apart and why you were considered. Utilize this feedback to refine your approach and enhance future interviews.

3. **Transform Setbacks into Opportunities:** Even if the board appointment does not materialize, your efforts need not be in vain. Request feedback, even if uncomfortable, to understand your strengths and areas for improvement. Acknowledge that the application process wasn't solely about securing a seat but also about building relationships. The research, connections, and knowledge gained during the process can lead to unforeseen opportunities. Reflect on whether the role was the right fit and leverage the experience to evolve and excel in future applications.

4. **Leverage Relationships:** Recognize the value of the relationships developed throughout the application process. These connections with current and past board directors, stakeholders, clients, and even competitors should be considered as 'weak ties' that hold substantial potential. While unsuccessful in one instance, these relationships, if maintained, can open doors to unexpected board opportunities in the future. Approximately 50% of all board appointments arise from such 'weak tie'

connections, emphasizing the importance of nurturing and leveraging these relationships. Make the interview process an extension of your professional network-building strategy.

5. **Relentless, Resilience, and Patience:** Embrace rejection as a natural part of your journey towards NED roles. Cultivating resilience and patience, along with an unwavering drive, is key to navigating the selection process. Setbacks are inevitable, but each one holds potential opportunities that can fuel your long-term growth and success. Make resilience and determination second nature, using every experience as a chance to learn and adapt.

Being rejected from a selection process does not always mean that you are not competent. Many times, it is simply that you are not the right fit for the organization, or they cannot see your value.

7.6. Due Diligence On The Organization

Before embracing a NED role, comprehensive due diligence is imperative. As much as the organization is conducting due diligence on you, you must also conduct due diligence on the organization. Consider the following aspects to ensure a well-informed decision:

1. Assessing Your Fit for the Position

- *Time Commitment:* Scrutinize the time commitment required for the role. Assess whether your schedule aligns with the demands of the position.
- *Networking Opportunities:* Evaluate if the position provides opportunities to expand your professional network.
- *Professional Growth:* Consider how the role contributes to your professional development and growth.
- *Compensation Structure:* Clarify how remuneration is structured and aligns with your expectations.
- *Legal and Ethical Responsibilities:* Understand the legal and ethical obligations associated with the role.

- *Vacancy Insights:* Investigate why the role is vacant, gaining insights into the organizational context.

2. Investigating the Organization

- *Organisation Profile:* Study the organization's profile, understanding its history, values, and strategic direction.
- *Conversations and Issues:* Analyse past, current, and potential issues through discussions, both internal and external.
- *Media Presence:* Analyze press releases, social media feeds, and trending news for a holistic understanding.
- *Financial Health:* Review Annual Financial Statements (AFS), Annual Reports, Investor Relations (IR) documents, past Board minutes, and other relevant reports.
- *Legal Standing:* Investigate any pending court cases or legal matters that may impact the organization's stability.

3. Scrutinizing Board Composition

- *Associations:* Evaluate whether you want to be associated with the other directors and management of the organization.
- *Alignment with Values:* Assess the alignment of your values and principles with those of the existing board members.
- *Diversity and Expertise:* Consider the diversity and expertise of the board and how it complements your skills and contributions.

4. Ethical Considerations

- *Values Alignment:* Ensure alignment between your personal and professional values and those of the organization.
- *Ethical Practices:* Investigate the organization's business practices and its commitment to ethical standards.

5. Future Viability

- *Growth Prospects:* Examine the organization's potential for future growth and its strategic vision.

- *Risk Management:* Assess the effectiveness of the organization's risk management practices.

Thorough due diligence ensures that your acceptance of a NED appointment is based on a comprehensive understanding of the organization and alignment with your professional objectives, values, and ethical considerations. Thus, by meticulously examining these facets, you position yourself to contribute effectively and thrive in your non-executive role.

It is important that the due diligence extends beyond the appointment. Once you have been appointed, you can get access to additional information and reports and, at times, during the induction period. Do not hesitate to revisit your initial decision to accept the appointment. It is common to find NEDs to resign within the first few weeks of the appointment as they get more information and reconsider the risk. Remember that it is your liability and professional reputation that is at stake. The bottom line is, can you afford the risk?

7.7. Board Compensation Structures

Board remuneration, or fees, are shaped by several factors, including:

- **Organization size**: Based on the company's staff size and/or revenue.
- **Industry and business complexity**: Boards overseeing complex industries face more challenging issues.
- **Meeting frequency**: The number of meetings a NED attends correlates with the level of effort required.
- **Time commitment**: The required time investment is proportional to the effort expected from the NED.
- **Experience and expertise**: A NED's remuneration is influenced by the value of their skills and experience, as determined by market demand.

Various fee structures exist, reflecting the diverse nature of organizations. Understanding these structures is crucial for aspiring and current NEDs. Here's an expanded overview:

❑ **Annual Retainer:** This structure involves a fixed annual retainer fee, providing directors with a steady income for their governance responsibilities. It is widely used across different sectors, especially in organizations with a stable financial structure.

❑ **Fees per Meeting (or per Hour):** Compensation is based on attendance, reflecting the time and effort invested in board and committee meetings. Common in organizations that require flexibility or have irregular meeting schedules.

❑ **Share/Equity-Based Fees:** Directors receive compensation in the form of organization shares or equity, aligning their interests with the organization's long-term success. Often used in growth-oriented organizations to foster a sense of ownership among NEDs.

❑ **Voluntary (Especially for Non-Profit):** Non-profit organizations may rely on voluntary professional contributions from NEDs who are passionate about the cause. Common in the non-profit sector, where directors may prioritize mission alignment over financial compensation.

❑ **Combination of the Above:** Organizations may adopt a hybrid approach, combining different fee structures to tailor compensation to the specific needs and circumstances of the board. This offers flexibility to meet the unique requirements of the organization and its directors.

Additional Considerations:

- *Travel and Other Disbursements:* Some organizations provide additional compensation for travel expenses and other disbursements incurred by NEDs.

- *Ad Hoc Meeting Fees:* Directors may receive extra compensation for participating in ad hoc or special meetings outside the regular schedule.

- *Annual Fee Preference for Larger Organizations:* Some larger organizations often prefer an annual fee structure, providing stability and predictability in compensation.

Understanding these fee structures empowers NEDs to make informed decisions about the roles they undertake. Factors such as organizational size, financial health, and the commitment expected from directors influence the choice of a particular fee structure. You can use this knowledge to align your compensation expectations with the prevailing industry standards and organizational practices.

7.8. Navigating Your First Board Meeting

As you embark on your journey as a NED, you will have your first board meeting. The following insights will serve as a compass, guiding you towards impactful contributions, effective collaboration, and learning as you participate in your inaugural board meeting. Here are essential tips to ensure a smooth and impactful first appearance:

- **Research and Connect:** Dive beyond basic understanding; look into the board members' professional histories, industry contributions, and potential shared interests. Establishing connections fosters a collaborative board environment.

- **Read the Board Papers/Pack:** Set aside time to study the board paper or board pack as you prepare for the meeting. Be clear about what is expected in the meeting based on the board pack. Study and research with the view of the required input to the meeting. Write notes and comments. Review your notes, refresh your memory, and perhaps get a new insight.

- **Review Agenda:** Go beyond surface-level comprehension. Review agenda details and supporting materials to cultivate a profound understanding. Pay attention to the key items, time-consuming items, and difficult items. This preparation boosts confidence and positions you as a prepared and engaged contributor.

- **Active Listening Mastery:** Mastering the art of active listening involves absorbing not just words but tones, unspoken cues, and diverse perspectives. If new information comes review and realign your inputs and comments to make them more relevant. By embracing this approach, you enrich discussions and demonstrate respect for varying viewpoints.

- **Question-Centric Engagement:** Transform discussions with a question-centric approach. Instead of immediate statements or judgments, pose insightful queries. This not only showcases engagement but also triggers comprehensive discussions, unraveling deeper insights.

- **Strategic Contribution Preparation:** Recognize your role as a unique contributor. Prepare to infuse fresh ideas into discussions, aligning with your expertise. Timing is key; contribute thoughtfully and seize appropriate moments to share your perspectives.

- **Conciseness with Impact:** Beyond brevity lies the art of impactful contribution. Ensure your insights are succinct, directly aligned with the agenda, and provide tangible value to the discussion. Elevate your contributions by focusing on relevance and clarity.

- **Learn From the Meeting:** Take notes of the contributions by other members and learn from them on how they engage on the issues. This will empower you for future board meetings.

- **Post-Meeting Debrief:** Maximize your learning curve by seeking a debrief with the Board Chair after the meeting. Uncover insights into your performance, grasp group dynamics, and explore areas for improvement. This proactive approach aids your continuous development.

- **Training:** Empower yourself by getting training in specific areas that you are lacking. For example, short courses in risk management, strategic oversight, audit, etc. These short courses will equip you to participate and contribute meaningfully in board meetings.

7.9. How to Read Board Papers

Reading board papers is a critical responsibility for board members, enabling you to fulfill your governance duties effectively. Board papers are essential documents and reports that provide crucial information for board members to make informed decisions and contribute effectively to the governance of an organization.

However, reading board papers can be a challenging task, especially for those who are new to the process. This section provides a step-by-step guide on how to develop a systematic approach to reading board papers efficiently, extracting the necessary information, and actively engaging in discussions during board meetings. With practice and attentiveness, you will enhance your ability to contribute meaningfully to the organization's success and make informed decisions for its future.

- **Prepare and Set the Stage:** Before immersing yourself in board papers, create an environment conducive to focused reading. Find a quiet space, free from distractions, where you can concentrate on the material. Ensure you have ample time to read and digest the documents without feeling rushed.

- **Familiarize Yourself with the Structure:** Understanding the structure of board papers helps you navigate through the information more efficiently. Generally, board papers consist of an agenda, minutes from the previous meeting, reports, and attachments. Browse through the documents to get a sense of the "state" of the organization and identify any critical sections that require immediate attention.

- **Review the Agenda:** The agenda provides an overview of the topics to be discussed during the board meeting. Pay close attention to the order of the agenda items, as it often reflects their relative importance. Use the agenda as a roadmap to guide your reading, ensuring you cover all the necessary sections in a logical sequence.

- **Analyze the Minutes:** The minutes from the previous meeting provide essential context and serve as a reminder of previous discussions and decisions. Review the minutes to refresh your memory and identify any pending action items or follow-up tasks. This will help you connect the current board papers with the ongoing board discussions.

- **Read Reports Carefully:** Reports form the core of the board papers and offer detailed information on various aspects of the organization's operations, finances, and performance. Take your time to read each report thoroughly, making notes of key points, trends, and concerns. Highlight any significant achievements or challenges that require further attention or discussion.

- **Pay Attention to Financial Statements:** Financial statements, such as income statements, balance sheets, and cash flow statements, provide critical insights into the organization's financial health. Familiarize yourself with the key financial metrics, analyze the trends, and identify any discrepancies or areas of concern. If necessary, seek clarification from the finance team or external auditors.

- **Assess Risks and Compliance:** Board papers often include risk assessments and compliance reports – highlighting potential threats and the organization's adherence to legal and regulatory requirements. Evaluate the identified risks and assess the adequacy of the proposed mitigation strategies. Ensure compliance reports indicate any areas of non-compliance and actions taken to address them.

- **Review Attachments and Appendices:** Attachments and appendices complement the reports and provide additional supporting information. While reading the board papers, refer to these attachments whenever necessary to gain a deeper understanding of the topics discussed. Pay attention to charts, graphs, and statistical data, as they can offer valuable insights into the organization's performance and trends.

- **Take Notes and Prepare Questions:** As you read through the board papers, take comprehensive notes to capture key information, issues, and your thoughts or concerns. These notes will be invaluable during the board meeting, facilitating informed discussions and decision-making. Prepare a list of relevant questions or requests for further clarification to ensure all your queries are addressed during the meeting.

- **Reflect and Discuss:** After reading the board papers, take some time to reflect on the information, analysis, and potential implications. Consider how the various reports and documents interrelate and shape the organization's overall strategy and direction. Engage in discussions with fellow board members and executives, sharing insights and perspectives to collectively contribute to the decision-making process.

7.10. Professional Development Strategies

As a NED, professional development is important for broadening your horizon and increasing your scope. Embracing the strategies below will not only enhance your professional development but also position you as an influential and sought-after NED.

- **Continual Skill Enhancement:** Elevate your skill set by immersing yourself in relevant and insightful content. Prioritize quality over quantity, focusing on materials that contribute to your expertise in governance. Intentionally curate your reading list to ensure every piece adds value to your knowledge base. Strive to become a recognized authority in your field through continuous learning.

- **Embrace Professionalism:** Take proactive steps to bolster your professional standing by obtaining relevant certifications and affiliating yourself with respected professional associations. These affiliations not only enhance your credibility but also provide a robust foundation for building a strategic network. Engage with like-minded professionals to foster collaborative relationships that can prove invaluable in your role as a NED.

- **Cultivate a Distinctive Personal Brand in Governance:** Distinguish yourself in the governance space by deliberately constructing a powerful personal brand. Leverage platforms such as LinkedIn to disseminate your thoughts, insights, and experiences. Author articles and books that showcase your expertise, ensuring that your content is targeted toward your desired audience. Actively seek opportunities to speak at industry forums, positioning yourself as the go-to authority in your domain. Craft your online presence with purpose, ensuring your engagements align with your professional goals.

- **Content Creation and Publication:** Generate and share valuable content to reinforce your personal brand. Craft thought-provoking articles, blog posts, and books that contribute to the discourse in governance. Utilize platforms like LinkedIn to disseminate your insights, effectively reaching your target audience. Thoughtful and intentional posting will not only establish you as an industry thought leader but also attract opportunities for collaboration and recognition.

- **Strategic Speaking Engagements:** Seize opportunities to share your expertise at various forums, positioning yourself as a subject matter expert. Engage in panel discussions, webinars, and conferences to showcase your knowledge and insights. When you actively participate in these events, you not only contribute to the broader industry dialogue but also enhance your visibility and credibility as a NED.

- **Network Building and Relationship Management:** Forge meaningful connections within the professional community. Actively participate in industry events, forums, and association meetings to build a robust network of peers and professionals. Nurturing these relationships can lead to collaborative opportunities, providing a platform for knowledge exchange and strategic alliances that can prove beneficial in your NED role.

7.11. Where to Start Searching

1. **Leverage Your Professional Network:** Initiate your journey into NED roles by tapping into your existing professional connections. Your network is a valuable asset, as those who are familiar with your capabilities can serve as advocates and recommend you for suitable opportunities. Cultivate relationships with colleagues, mentors, and

industry peers to establish a solid foundation for your directorial aspirations.

2. **Explore Advertised Vacancies:** Keep a vigilant eye on various channels for advertised NED opportunities. Regularly scan newspapers, dedicated websites, and online platforms where organizations frequently post vacancies. Staying informed about these openings broadens your scope and allows you to proactively pursue roles that align with your skills and interests.

3. **Uncover Opportunities in Non-Profit Organizations:** Expand your horizons by researching roles in non-profit entities, which often present diverse and fulfilling NED opportunities. Consider involvement in:

- *Professional Associations:* Join boards of industry-specific associations as you connect with like-minded professionals and discover potential directorial roles.
- *School Governing Bodies (SGB):* Contribute to the governance of educational institutions, providing valuable oversight and strategic direction.
- *Special Interest Groups:* Participate in and join boards of groups focused on specific areas of interest, where your expertise can make a meaningful impact.
- *Community Engagement Forums:* Engage with and join boards of community-based organizations, such as community police forums, local business forums, and Homeowners Associations (HOAs), to contribute to local governance.
- *Committees Within and Outside Your Organisation:* Explore committee roles within your current organization and extend your reach outside by participating in committees of other organizations around you. This can offer exposure to different industries and expand your network.
- *Community Development Associations:* Contribute to the growth and development of your community by becoming involved in

associations dedicated to community welfare and development. Join the board and committees.

In a nutshell, actively participating in non-profit organizations helps you not only contribute to societal well-being but also position yourself for meaningful NED opportunities. Embark on your NED journey armed with these strategies, and you'll be well on your way to securing roles that align with your expertise and passion.

8.1. The Well-Rounded Director

Wellness, self-perception, executive presence, and dressing play integral roles in shaping a director's success and impact. As a director, your well-being, both physically and mentally, is paramount as it directly influences your ability to handle challenges and maintain sustained performance. A director's self-perception contributes significantly to leadership effectiveness, influencing confidence, decision-making, and the ability to inspire teams.

Executive presence encompasses a combination of gravitas, communication skills, and a commanding demeanor, all crucial for earning respect and influencing stakeholders. Additionally, a director's dressing style goes beyond mere aesthetics; it serves as a visual representation of professionalism, attention to detail, and alignment with organizational values. Collectively, these elements create a harmonious blend of personal and professional attributes, enhancing a director's capability to lead, inspire, and drive success within the organization.

In the next section, we will look at how to navigate and leverage these factors.

8.2. Nurturing a Director's Wellness

One of my mentors once said, '*I have never seen a millionaire who is obese.*' He was pointing out that your health challenges restrict your progress toward success. Treat your health and personal wellness as a risk that must be managed.

Achieving optimal well-being is paramount for effective leadership and decision-making. Let's briefly look into the multifaceted dimensions of directors' wellness and health, emphasizing the importance of fostering healthy habits across the mind, heart, and body.

a) **Cultivating a Resilient Mind through Mental Wellness:**
When necessary, directors are encouraged to seek professional counseling to manage stress, enhance resilience, and maintain mental clarity. Foster a Good Social Life, with a strong support network, as maintaining healthy relationships can contribute to mental well-being.

b) **Nurturing a Healthy Heart Through Emotional Intelligence:**
Emotional Well-being is important for a director. If necessary, extend counseling services to address emotional challenges, promoting emotional intelligence and resilience. Avoid Toxic Environments. Ensure that the workplace culture prioritizes positivity and discourages toxic behaviors, safeguarding directors' emotional health.

c) **Sustaining a Fit Body through Physical Wellness Initiatives:**
Incorporate regular physical exercise into your normal schedule. Embrace physical activity as an integral part of your routine, fostering improved stamina, focus, and overall well-being. Be mindful of nutritional intake. Develop conscious eating habits, promoting a well-balanced diet that supports physical health.

It is imperative to prioritize directors' well-being comprehensively. This way, you can foster healthy habits across the mind, heart, and body, which, in turn, empowers you to lead with resilience, emotional intelligence, and physical vitality. This holistic approach not only benefits you but also contributes to a thriving and sustainable corporate culture.

8.3. Self-Perception Shapes Your Leadership Success

Your thought processes are directly tied to your leadership style, playing a critical role in shaping your path to success. How you see yourself serves as the mirror through which you assess your leadership capabilities. Likewise, others use this same mirror to judge your leadership effectiveness.

This section explores the deep connection between self-perception and cognitive approaches, highlighting how these mental patterns deeply influence leadership behaviors.

Self-Image (How do you view yourself?): A leader's self-image profoundly impacts their leadership style and personal growth. Cultivating a positive self-image helps foster traits like confidence, ambition, and resilience, which are vital for leadership.

Perception of Leadership (What is your view of leadership?): Your understanding of what leadership entails shapes how you lead. This perception influences your professional qualities and key leadership attributes such as trust, vision, and empathy.

Leadership traits shaped by self-image and leadership perception include:

- **Building Trustworthiness:** Your self-image and view of leadership affect your ability to establish and maintain trust within your team and organization.
- **Shaping Visionary Leadership:** Thought patterns influence how leaders develop and communicate their vision for the future.
- **Cultivating Empathy:** Cognitive frameworks impact a leader's capacity for empathy and understanding, key traits for effective leadership.
- **Strengthening Resilience:** Your mental approach plays a crucial role in building resilience and navigating challenges effectively.

- **Fostering Positive Social Connections:** Enhancing sociability is possible by positively shaping your self-image and leadership schema.
- **Promoting Growth through Perseverance:** By identifying, challenging, and reshaping important beliefs and patterns, leaders inspire growth and productivity within their teams.
- **Enhancing Collaborative Leadership:** Mental frameworks significantly promote collaboration and communication within leadership teams.
- **The Mind as the Foundation of Leadership:** Leadership structures are rooted in cognitive processes, emphasizing the central role of thought patterns in effective leadership.

Leadership excellence is intricately connected to the thought patterns that govern our self-perception and understanding of leadership roles. Recognizing, analyzing, and evolving your self-image and idea of leadership fosters a mindset that positively influences not only your own growth but also the success of your teams and organizations.

8.4. Mastering Executive Presence

The ability to exude confidence, composure, and the capacity to engage and inspire others is encapsulated in the concept of Executive Presence. Let's look into the different aspects of Executive Presence, exploring the key traits and strategies that contribute to projecting a compelling and influential leadership image.

What is Executive Presence? It is the art of projecting confidence and composure while engaging others in a manner that inspires them to take action. Executive Presence encompasses various elements, including body language, voice projection, empathy, and vulnerability.

According to Forbes magazine, there are 7 traits of executive presence, all beginning with the letter "C". They are Composure, Connection, Charisma, Confidence, Credibility, Clarity, and Conciseness. It involves inspiring Confidence:

- *Among Subordinates:* Being a leader that subordinates willingly follow, recognizing the leader they want to emulate.
- *Among Peers:* Establishing capability and reliability among peers, fostering a collaborative and respectful professional environment.
- *Among Senior Leaders:* Demonstrating potential for significant achievements, capturing the attention and respect of senior leadership.

Here are more details about the 7 Cs of Executive Presence:

1) **Composure:** Composure is the ability to stay calm and in control, grounded in self-awareness and emotional intelligence. This skill encompasses several components: self-awareness, which involves understanding your own emotions and reactions; understanding others, which includes the capacity to empathize and recognize emotions in those around you; emotional control, which is about managing and regulating your emotional responses across different situations; and adaptability, the flexibility to adjust your reactions based on the emotional signals of others.

2) **Connection:** Connection involves building and maintaining rapport and relationships by adapting communication styles to engage others effectively. This includes engaging in inclusive and comfortable communication tailored to the audience, being self-aware of one's own communication style, recognizing personal challenges, and adapting to others by understanding and adjusting to their communication styles for more effective engagement.

3) **Charisma:** Charisma is developed by drawing others in through a genuine focus on them, strong listening skills, and being fully present in the moment. It begins with making others feel valued and important during interactions, demonstrating strong listening by actively engaging in conversations without distractions. By staying

attentive and offering undivided attention, one can cultivate the charisma that fosters meaningful connections.

4) **Confidence:** Confidence is communicated through a combination of physical presence, vocal modulation, and professional appearance. It involves maintaining good posture, steady eye contact, and appropriate facial expressions to project assurance. Vocal modulation is equally important, ensuring that the pitch, volume, and pace of speech align with the message. Additionally, a well-chosen wardrobe that fits the expectations of the role and organization reinforces confidence and credibility.

5) **Credibility:** Credibility is built by delivering high-quality content and using precise language that avoids common detractors of credibility. This involves crafting impactful, well-thought-out messages while steering clear of bad grammar, filler language, and minimizers, all of which can undermine the strength and clarity of communication. Focusing on these elements effectively establishes trust and authority.

6) **Clarity:** Clarity is a key element of strong communication and presence, demonstrated by the ability to convey a message in 10 words or less. Mastering clarity involves articulating concise, focused messages that command attention and leave no room for ambiguity.

7) **Conciseness:** Conciseness is about staying on point and delivering content that is relevant to the listener's needs without unnecessary elaboration. By avoiding verbosity, the message remains focused and impactful, ensuring that communication is efficient and effective.

Executive Presence is an attainable trait for Non-Executive Directors (NEDs), achievable through personal reflection, deliberate practice, and targeted coaching. Thus, understanding and embodying the essential elements of Executive Presence elevates your leadership impact, gaining the trust, respect, and admiration of your colleagues, subordinates, and senior leaders alike.

8.5. Unveiling the Power of Dressing for Success

To assume that dressing is not important is to make a grave mistake, as you will be judged by how you dress, and the first impression has a long-lasting effect. The importance of dressing for success extends beyond mere aesthetics. Let's look at the transformative impact of intentional attire, emphasizing how clothing choices can positively influence performance, shape perceptions, impact career trajectories, and align with organizational cultures. Here are some considerations for your attire;

1) **Performance Enhancement:**
   The clothing choices have a psychological effect on your performance. Certain specific attire can boost confidence, focus, and overall effectiveness. A polished professional appearance can enhance a director's credibility and authority in boardroom settings.

2) **Perception Management:**
   There is a correlation between clothing choices and your first impressions. Your attire plays a critical role in shaping perceptions among colleagues, stakeholders, and peers. On the other hand, as a director, you represent the organization's brand through your attire, serving as ambassadors of the organization's values and standards.

3) **Career Direction and Professional Growth:**
   Dress for the Future. Adopt a forward-looking approach by dressing for the role that you aspire to attain, emphasizing the link between professional image and career progression. Aligning your attire with your career goals can positively influence opportunities, promotions, and networking prospects.

4) **Body-Appropriate Attire:**
   Choose clothing that complements your body type and shape, promoting a professional and confident appearance. Ensure that you

are comfortable in your clothing choices, as discomfort can impact focus and overall performance during board engagements.

5) **Confidence and Well-Being:**
The psychological benefit of wearing clothes that make you feel confident and comfortable is that they foster a positive mindset. Confidence in appearance can translate into assertive leadership and successful decision-making.

6) **Aligning with Organizational Culture and Dress Code:**
Try to understand organizational norms and be cognizant of the dress code and cultural expectations within your organization. Find a harmonious balance between personal style and adherence to organizational norms.

7) **Dressing as Brand Representation:**
Your clothing communicates values. As a director, your role includes being a brand ambassador. Your attire needs to reflect and uphold the organization's values. External stakeholders perceive the organization based on the professional image projected by its directors.

8) **The Motto is 'Dress for the Role You Want':**
Dress like a visionary and lead by example. Directors should dress for the role they aspire to occupy, showcasing a proactive and goal-oriented mindset. This example of setting a standard for professional dress in the boardroom can inspire a culture of professionalism and purpose throughout the organization.

By intentionally approaching attire choices, directors can harness the transformative power of clothing to positively impact performance, career trajectories, and organizational perceptions. Serving as brand representatives, you wield the ability to influence not only your personal success but also the overall image and standing of the organizations that you serve.

8.6. Navigating Boardroom Realities

As you embark on your NED leadership journey, cultivating self-awareness becomes a compass guiding you through the intricate terrain of the boardroom. This section looks at the critical aspects of awareness, addressing the allure of charisma, the different approaches to wealth, the pitfalls of pride, and the delicate nature of professional relationships.

1) **The Attraction and Pitfalls of Charisma:**
   Be aware of charismatic magnetism and possible unintended consequences. Acknowledge the allure of charisma, attracting attention and admiration within boardroom dynamics. Moths and bugs are drawn to a charismatic flame, underscoring the potential drawbacks and pitfalls associated with magnetic personalities.

2) **Focus on Impact and Influence, not Money and Wealth:**
   Go beyond a narrow focus on money and wealth, redirecting your attention towards the broader spheres of impact and influence. Build a legacy that lasts generations: Build lasting impact by leveraging your positions to effect positive change, leaving a meaningful legacy.

3) **The Danger of Pride:**
   Strive for collective intelligence. It is not wise to be the smartest person in the room. There is a high risk associated with pride, particularly the belief in being the smartest person in the room. Advocate for a collaborative leadership approach, leveraging the diverse expertise of the board for more effective decision-making.

4) **Vigilance and Clarity when Navigating Relationships:**
   Management of your relationship dynamics. Acknowledge the intricate nature of professional relationships within the boardroom and the need for vigilance. Develop strategies for navigating potential conflicts, ensuring that relationships do not compromise the integrity of the board or individual directors.

5) **Setting Clear Boundaries:**
   Clear communication is important. Set boundaries and maintain transparency in interactions with fellow directors and stakeholders. Strive for the establishment of clear professional boundaries, fostering a healthy and respectful environment within the board.

6) **Continuous Reflection:**
   Cultivating a culture of self-awareness is vital. Be proactive by adopting an ongoing process of self-reflection as a tool to understand your strengths, weaknesses, and impact on others.

7) **Integrating Lessons Learned: Lifelong Learning:**
   Extract valuable wisdom from your past experiences. Your past experiences can provide value to your learning, both positive and challenging, to enhance self-awareness and leadership effectiveness. Seek mentorship and guidance, leveraging the collective wisdom of seasoned leaders to refine your own approaches.

Self-awareness emerges as an invaluable tool for navigating the multifaceted dynamics of the boardroom. Remaining mindful of the dual nature of charisma, embracing a holistic view of wealth, mitigating the risks associated with pride, and fostering healthy relationships will help a director chart a course toward impactful and influential leadership. Continuous self-reflection becomes the cornerstone of sustained growth, enabling you to cultivate a holistic understanding of yourself and your role.

9.1. Introduction

This chapter looks at various ways that you can unleash your full potential as a Non-Executive Director (NED), by identifying your uniqueness in the context of your society, identifying tools and resources, identifying opportunities, and crafting a unique strategy that advances your non-executive career. In the later sections, we will look at how to position yourself to maintain momentum and grow in all circumstances, in any environment, at all times.

9.2. Navigating Your Uniqueness

Recognizing and understanding your social, economic, and societal profile is paramount for effective leadership. Let's investigate the concept of intersectionality, highlighting the unique circumstances everyone brings to the boardroom based on various social identities. By acknowledging the effects of factors such as gender, race, ethnicity, sexual orientation, economic class, religion, disability, body weight, physical appearance, origin, and immigration status, you can cultivate a holistic understanding of your societal advantages and disadvantages, and craft the appropriate board career strategy.

Acknowledging and navigating your social, economic, and societal profile is a foundational aspect of effective leadership in Non-Executive Directorship.

You cannot change the society and the way it views you. However, you can create a strategy to manage, minimize or even overcome the negative effects and/or maximize the positive effects. Here are some considerations;

1) **Social Identities as Variables:** Unpack the diversity of social factors that shape you, acknowledging the multifaceted nature of personal circumstances. View your social identities as intersecting variables, recognizing the complex interplay of advantages and disadvantages.

2) **Recognize your Advantages and Disadvantages:** Acknowledge social advantages, such as gender, race, or economic class, which can confer privileges to certain individuals. At the same time, understand the statistical evidence that highlights the additional effort required for those facing disadvantages.

3) **Effort Across the Spectrum:** Being advantaged doesn't eliminate the need for effort, but it presents different challenges and responsibilities. Recognize the shared responsibility of fostering inclusive environments, regardless of privilege or disadvantage.

4) **Crafting Personal Strategies:** Conduct a thorough self-assessment, mapping out how various social factors may impact your experience in the boardroom. Tailor a personal career strategy that considers intersectionality to foster a more inclusive and empathetic leadership approach.

5) **Societal Dynamics:** Societal norms and biases can contribute to disadvantages for certain individuals based on their social identities. Intersectionality can influence access to opportunities and career advancement within the broader societal context.

6) **Personal Empowerment:** Empowerment comes from understanding your intersectional identity, enabling you to navigate challenges with resilience. By embracing intersectionality, contribute to a collective impact that promotes diversity, equity, and inclusion within the boardroom.

9.3. Framework for Unleashing Your Full Potential

Unlocking your full potential as a NED requires a strategic approach that encompasses three critical dimensions: harnessing available tools and resources, cultivating a resilient mindset, attitude, and wisdom, and astutely identifying and leveraging opportunities within the environment.

You must consider three pivotal areas for a well-rounded approach to leadership: the arsenal of available tools and resources, the cultivation of a mindset fortified with the right attitude and wisdom, and the careful evaluation of opportunities within the environment. Let's look at the significance of these dimensions and emphasize the importance of drawing inspiration from great leaders and diverse sources.

1) **Instruments and Resources at your Disposal**
   Success is deeply intertwined with the strategic consideration of available tools, the cultivation of a resilient mindset, and the astute identification of opportunities.

   - **Tangible & Intangible Assets:** Conduct a comprehensive assessment of both your tangible resources (financial and technological) and your intangible resources (networks and expertise) available to you, recognizing your multifaceted nature. The six-capital model shows diverse sources of resources for value creation that contribute to the overall wealth of a person and organization. As you deploy resources, maximize impact and effectiveness in decision-making.

   - *Natural,* **Manmade***, and Modified Assets:* Leveraging the natural resources around you. Acknowledge your natural attributes such as birth, physical appearance, family background, and inherent gifts, emphasizing the power of embracing your innate qualities. Some resources are manmade, and others may have to be modified. Explore the impact of education, training, development, and proactive modifications in countering disadvantages and enhancing capabilities.

- *Developing a Detailed Plan:* Develop a detailed plan for all your resources, including financial, time, capabilities (skills, gifts, talents, knowledge), and professional networks. Emphasize the strategic allocation of resources to optimize value creation and achieve your personal and organizational goals.

2) **Your Mindset, Attitude, and Wisdom**
- **Perception, Resilience, and Creativity:** Cultivating a visionary perception sets the foundation for effective leadership and decision-making. Differentiate between devotion and commitment, emphasizing the importance of resilience in navigating challenges and setbacks. Advocate for a mindset that embraces change, fostering creativity and innovation in adapting to evolving circumstances. Your mindset plays a critical role in effective leadership. Foster a resilient and growth-oriented mindset. Your attitude determines the quality of your decision-making process and the wisdom gained through experience and continuous learning.

- **Lifelong Learning:** Commit to a lifelong learning journey, incorporating a continual process of unlearning and relearning. A life of learning contributes to personal and professional growth, enhancing wisdom and adaptability.

- **Develop an Improvement Plan:** Develop a detailed plan for improving your mindset, attitude, and wisdom. The emphasis should be on regular self-assessment and reflection to identify areas for improvement and growth.

3) **Opportunities at Your Disposal**
- **Dynamic Nature of Opportunities:** Opportunities vary by time, context, and personal needs, necessitating a dynamic and

adaptive approach. Opportunities can arise naturally, be manmade, or be influenced, providing a spectrum of potential avenues for growth.

- **Identify and Leverage Opportunities:** Foster a proactive mindset in identifying opportunities, whether they come naturally, are created, or can be influenced to align with personal goals. Adopt a strategic decision-making process to capitalize on identified opportunities, emphasizing the significance of timing and readiness.

- **Develop an Opportunity Plan:** Develop a plan to identify and leverage available opportunities within your environment. Agility and adaptability are important elements when approaching perceived opportunities, recognizing that the approach to opportunities is as crucial as their identification. Thoroughly evaluate your environment for potential opportunities, trends, and challenges. Be adaptable and responsive to the evolving opportunities within your sector.

4) **Learn from Great Leaders and Outstanding Personalities**
   By drawing inspiration from the stories of great leaders, both on-screen and in literature, you can enrich your perspective and collect valuable lessons to navigate the complexities of your role.

- Study the life stories of great leaders through biographies and documentaries. There is the transformative power of studying inspirational leaders who have overcome challenges and achieved greatness. Read biographies and leadership magazines that can become sources of wisdom for you.

- As for me, movies like "Tetris," "The Banker," "Stein Heist," and "Becoming Buffet" carry valuable life lessons and showcase inspirational leadership principles. My favorite inspiring stories include stars like Michael Jackson, James Brown, and Arnold

Schwarzenegger, given their humble beginnings and passion-driven journeys.

5) **Empowerment is the Only Way Forward:**
   - Someone once said, *'The best revenge is success.'* This mantra serves as a powerful motivator, propelling leaders towards continuous self-improvement and heightened achievements. Focus on self-improvement and achieving excellence. Overcoming your adversaries through intelligence and self-improvement contributes to resilient and empowered leadership.

Unlocking your full potential as a NED demands a holistic and strategic approach across available tools and resources, mindset, attitude, and wisdom, as well as the identification and leveraging of opportunities. As such, by meticulously developing plans for each dimension and fostering a continuous learning mindset, you can navigate the complexities of your role with resilience, innovation, and strategic acumen. This comprehensive framework provides a roadmap for continuous improvement and success.

9.4. Framework for Navigating Life's Seasons

Life and careers, akin to the changing seasons, unfold in distinct phases, each presenting unique challenges and opportunities. As stewards of governance, you, as a NED, can benefit from crafting strategic approaches tailored to the different seasons of your professional and personal life. Let's investigate the metaphor of life's seasons, providing insights and strategies to guide you through the diverse phases of your journey.

The ultimate success in business and career comes from taking a strategic approach that minimizes the impairments of each season and, at times, turns misfortunes into opportunities. The duration of a season is not defined, and so is the sequence of the seasons. Whichever season you are in, remember that the seasons will turn. Are you ready for the next season?

1. Embracing Good Times in Summer

Summer seasons are associated with peak performance. Maximize your potential during the "Summer" phase of your career, leveraging opportunities for growth and impact. Set ambitious goals and expand professional horizons during periods of success. Use the positive momentum of summer to build resilience, anticipating and preparing for potential challenges in future seasons. Develop and foster positive relationships and networking during good times, fostering a supportive professional community.

2. Navigating the Uncertainty of Autumn

Acknowledge the uncertainties that come with the "Autumn" phase and stress the importance of maintaining a realistic outlook. Use this season for skill enhancement and continuous learning, preparing for potential challenges ahead. Craft strategies that look beyond immediate challenges, prepare for the future and position yourself for resilience. In this season, crisis management skills are important. Remain composed and proactive in the face of adversity.

3. Enduring Tough Times Across the Winter

Endurance is required to successfully navigate the "Winter" phase, with reliance on resilience and adaptability. Do not stop ongoing learning and skill development as you navigate tough times and prepare for the eventual transition to a new season. Seek mentorship and support networks during challenging seasons, leveraging the wisdom and experience of others. Develop a culture of collaboration within the board and the executive, fostering unity in facing adversity.

4. Embracing Renewal in Spring

The emergence of "Spring" is a time for renewal and opportunities, a sign of positive things to come. Proactively seize emerging opportunities, leveraging lessons learned from previous seasons. Strategically position yourself for the next phase of your career, focusing on reinvention and adaptation. Pay it forward by offering mentorship to others and contributing to a supportive professional community.

Understanding and strategically navigating the seasons of life and career is paramount. By adopting proactive approaches during the good times, preparing for uncertainties, weathering tough phases, and embracing renewal, directors can build resilience, continuously learn, and position themselves for sustained success. This metaphorical framework provides a holistic guide for you to embrace the dynamism of your role with wisdom and strategic foresight.

10.1. Sustaining Motivation with a Positive Mindset

The journey to securing Non-Executive Director (NED) positions is not without challenges. It is crucial to embrace both successes and setbacks, as well as develop resilience, patience, and a resilient mindset to navigate the ups and downs.

Maintaining a positive mindset is indispensable for you to secure a NED role. The journey towards obtaining a board seat can be challenging, particularly when confronted with rejection and disappointment. You must cultivate a positive mindset to weather such challenges and stay motivated throughout the process.

1) Key Characteristics of a Positive Mindset:
- Embrace an optimistic mindset that encourages proactive efforts and risk-taking rather than assuming that endeavors will go unrewarded.
- Practice acceptance by acknowledging that outcomes may not always align with expectations. Transform these experiences into opportunities for personal growth and continuous learning.
- Cultivate resilience, the ability to bounce back from adversity, disappointment, and failure without succumbing to defeat. Recognize that resilience is a vital leadership skill, especially for those aspiring to become board directors.

2) How to Sustain Positivity and Motivation in Board Pursuits:
- Stay optimistic and goal-oriented. Maintain an optimistic outlook and persistently work towards your board aspirations, even in the face of rejection. View setbacks as stepping stones toward eventual success.
- Visualize success and persistence. Visualize yourself succeeding in a board role, and persistently refine your skills, and accumulate

relevant experience. Consistent improvement is key to positioning yourself as a compelling candidate.

- Avoid negativity. Guard against negativity and disgruntlement, as they can adversely impact your language and attitude. Projecting a positive demeanor is crucial for building constructive relationships in the boardroom.

- Maintain faith in yourself. Foster self-belief and trust that the right board opportunity will present itself. Confidence in your abilities contributes significantly to your attractiveness as a candidate.

As a prospective member of the board of directors, you should recognize that resilient teams are built by resilient leaders. The development of resilience is not only a personal imperative but also a leadership requirement. As you aspire to join a board, consider resilience as a core skill to hone and showcase.

10.2. Way Forward

Embarking on the journey to become a NED involves a strategic and well-thought-out approach. To summarize the key steps:

- *Understand the Director's Role:* Gain a comprehensive understanding of the responsibilities and expectations of a director. Confirm your genuine interest in contributing to corporate governance.

- *Acquire Necessary Knowledge, Skills, and Experience:* Invest in continuous learning and development to stay abreast of industry trends and regulations. Cultivate the essential skills required for effective board leadership.

- *Network with the Right People:* Establish meaningful connections within the corporate and governance spheres. Leverage relationships with influencers and decision-makers.

- *Proactive Networking:* Communicate your interest in board appointments. Dedicate time each week to network, seeking opportunities for improvement.

- *Build Your Personal Brand:* Develop a strong presence in the corporate governance space. Cultivate a positive and distinctive image that reflects your expertise and values.
- *Craft a Compelling Director's Portfolio:* Create an impressive CV, profile, and narrative showcasing your qualifications and achievements. Perfect your pitch to articulate your value proposition effectively.
- *Stay Informed About Board Vacancies:* Keep a keen eye on board vacancies through various channels. Actively pursue opportunities aligned with your skills and aspirations.
- *Targeted Search:* Identify a list of organizations aligned with your goals. Monitor reputable platforms where board positions are advertised.
- *Know Your Value:* Understand and articulate your unique value proposition. Constantly update your board profile to reflect evolving skills and experiences.
- *Prepare Thoroughly for Interviews:* Approach interviews with meticulous preparation, demonstrating a deep understanding of the organization. Showcase your readiness to contribute to the board's success.
- *Conduct Due Diligence on Organizations:* Investigate potential board positions and organizations thoroughly. Ensure alignment with your values and assess the organization's financial health and reputation.

10.3.   Final Words

In your pursuit of becoming a NED, keep these principles in mind:
- *Value of Experience:* While experience is valuable, practicality is indispensable in the boardroom.
- *Choose the Best Path:* Opt for the most effective route to the top, not necessarily the easiest one.
- *Perception Shapes Reality:* Your perception influences your future; approach opportunities with a positive mindset.

- *Leverage Networks:* Your network is more extensive than you think; leverage it wisely.
- *Facilitate Help:* Make it easy for others to assist you by maintaining positive relationships.
- *Kindness Matters:* Be considerate and gracious to those you encounter on your journey.
- *Define Your Success:* Measure success on your terms, not by external standards.
- *Enjoy the Journey:* Life is a long journey; savor and learn from every experience along the way.

A positive mindset is not just a personal asset but a fundamental element in the journey towards a NED role. Embrace optimism, practice acceptance, and cultivate resilience to navigate the challenges inherent in the pursuit of board leadership. By staying positive and focused, you enhance your chances of securing the right board opportunity for your unique skills and contributions.

10.4. Invitation to Make a Difference

I hope you enjoyed this book and it has added value to your development journey as a NED.

- Post on LinkedIn a photo of yourself with the book & get a 1-year subscription to board vacancies (Terms and Conditions apply). Do not forget to tag me on the post.

- The author is available to speak on these and related issues.

- Anvil Advisory is available for any board development, training, and corporate governance consulting, including ISO37000 certification.

* Let's connect :

- LinkedIn – or,
- Visit my website -

* If you have questions or comments, please connect with me

Non-Executive Director (NED) CV Sample One

Name: [Your Name]
Certified Director® | Corporate Governance Specialist | Non-Executive Director
Contact Information:

Phone: [Your Phone Number]   LinkedIn: [Your LinkedIn Profile URL]
Email: [Your Email Address]   Location: [Your City, Country]

❑ **Professional Profile**

A results-oriented Non-Executive Director with over [X] years of experience providing strategic oversight and governance leadership across various industries, including [List key industries]. Skilled in corporate governance, risk management, and boardroom dynamics, I am passionate about promoting sustainability, innovation, and ethical leadership. Recognized for my ability to balance risk and opportunity, ensuring robust governance practices that drive sustainable growth.

❑ **Core Competencies**

- Corporate Governance
- Strategic Leadership
- Risk Management & Compliance
- Stakeholder Engagement
- Financial Oversight
- ESG (Environmental, Social, and Governance)
- Succession Planning
- Audit & Remuneration Committees
- Mergers & Acquisitions
- Regulatory Compliance

❑ **Board Experience**

Non-Executive Director
Company Name – [City, Country]
[Month, Year] – Present

126

- Provide strategic advice and governance oversight to help steer the company in achieving long-term objectives.
- Chair/serve on committees such as the Audit Committee and Risk Committee, ensuring strong financial and risk controls.
- Contribute to succession planning, executive compensation policies, and ESG initiatives.
- Work closely with stakeholders to align corporate strategy with market trends and shareholder expectations.

Non-Executive Director
Company Name – [City, Country]
[Month, Year] – [Month, Year]
- Actively contributed to the company's strategic direction, focusing on corporate governance, financial oversight, and risk management.
- Engaged in reviewing and approving corporate financial statements and annual budgets.
- Championed ESG and sustainability projects, promoting ethical and responsible business practices.

❑ **Executive Experience**

Managing Director
Company Name – [City, Country]
[Month, Year] – Present
- Lead a consulting firm specializing in infrastructure consulting, project management training, and corporate governance advisory.
- Oversee operations, strategic planning, and business development, ensuring continued profitability and growth.
- Mentor and coach aspiring directors through the Director Mentorship Programme.

[Previous Executive Role]
Company Name – [City, Country]
[Month, Year] – [Month, Year]

- Led corporate governance projects, developed risk management frameworks, and managed regulatory compliance for [Industry].

❑ **Education & Certifications**

- **Master of Business Administration (MBA)** – [University Name], [Year]
- **Honours Degree in Civil Engineering** – [University Name], [Year]
- **Certified Director®** – [Issuing Organization], [Year]
- **Project Management Professional (PMP)®** – [Issuing Organization], [Year]

❑ **Professional Affiliations**

- Member, Institute of Directors (IoD)
- Member, Corporate Governance Network
- Member, Project Management Institute (PMI)

❑ **Key Achievements**

- **Boardroom Transformation:** Successfully introduced an ESG strategy for [Company], leading to a [X]% improvement in sustainability metrics within two years.
- **Risk Management Leadership:** Played a key role in establishing a comprehensive risk framework that reduced operational risks by [X]% at [Company].
- **Financial Oversight:** Led audit committee that improved transparency and compliance, resulting in successful external audits for [X] consecutive years.

❑ **Publications & Speaking Engagements**

- **Author,** *Roadmap to Non-Executive Directorship – The Essential Handbook*
- Featured speaker at [Conference/Event Name], presenting on corporate governance and risk management strategies.

❑ **References**

Available upon request.

Non-Executive Director (NED) CV Sample Two

[Your Name]
Certified Director® | Corporate Governance Expert | Non-Executive Director
Contact Information
Phone: [Your Phone Number] | Email: [Your Email Address] | LinkedIn: [Your LinkedIn Profile]
Location: [Your City, Country]

❏ Board Profile

A seasoned Non-Executive Director with over [X] years of experience across diverse industries including [mention key industries]. I bring deep expertise in corporate governance, risk management, financial oversight, and sustainability. Known for providing strategic guidance and holding executive teams accountable, I ensure robust governance frameworks that drive long-term organizational success. Adept at navigating complex regulatory landscapes, I also prioritize ethical decision-making and the integration of Environmental, Social, and Governance (ESG) principles. My contributions on boards have consistently led to improved risk management, stakeholder relations, and sustainable growth.

❏ Value Proposition

As an experienced NED, I combine strategic vision, governance acumen, and financial literacy to offer impactful leadership at the board level. I excel at:

- **Corporate Governance & Risk Management**: I have a proven track record of enhancing governance structures and reducing enterprise risk. For instance, I led the introduction of a comprehensive risk management framework that cut operational risks by [X]% at [Company].

- **Financial Oversight & Audit**: With hands-on experience in finance and audit committees, I am skilled at scrutinizing financial reports, ensuring transparency, and maintaining regulatory compliance. At [Company], I chaired the audit committee that secured [X] years of consecutive clean audits.

- **Sustainability & ESG Leadership**: Passionate about sustainability, I spearheaded an ESG initiative that improved corporate sustainability metrics by [X]% and led to a notable increase in investor confidence.
- **Stakeholder Engagement & Communication**: I bring strong communication and interpersonal skills, successfully managing relationships with shareholders, regulators, and other stakeholders, ensuring alignment with the company's strategic objectives.

❑ **Board & Committee Experience**

Non-Executive Director
Company Name – [City, Country]
[Month, Year] – Present
- Serve as an independent board member providing strategic oversight, governance, and risk management.
- Chair the [Audit/Remuneration/Risk] Committee and member of the Nomination Committee.
- Key achievements: Drove board discussions around [specific initiative], resulting in [specific outcome].

Non-Executive Director
Company Name – [City, Country]
[Month, Year] – [Month, Year]
- Provided governance guidance during a critical organizational restructuring that saw a [X]% improvement in operational efficiency.
- Led the development of a new governance policy that strengthened compliance with regulatory standards.

Chair, Audit Committee
Company Name – [City, Country]
[Month, Year] – [Month, Year]
- Oversaw financial reporting, risk management, and audit processes, ensuring adherence to the highest standards of corporate governance.

- Key achievements: Played a pivotal role in improving financial transparency and securing external audit approvals.

❑ Executive Experience

Managing Director
Company Name – [City, Country]
[Month, Year] – Present

- Provide leadership in infrastructure consulting, project management, and corporate governance advisory services.
- Mentor and develop emerging leaders through the Director Mentorship Programme, helping them secure board positions.

[Previous Executive Role]
Company Name – [City, Country]
[Month, Year] – [Month, Year]

- Led [specific function or department] to deliver on [specific project or goal], increasing [revenue/efficiency/success metric] by [X]% during tenure.

❑ Qualifications & Certifications

- **Master of Business Administration (MBA)** – [University Name], [Year]
- **Honours Degree in Civil Engineering** – [University Name], [Year]
- **Certified Director®** – [Issuing Organization], [Year]
- **Project Management Professional (PMP)®** – [Issuing Organization], [Year]
- **Chartered Director (CDir)** – [Issuing Organization], [Year]
- **Diploma in Corporate Governance** – [Institution Name], [Year]

❑ Professional Affiliations

- Member, Institute of Directors (IoD)
- Member, Corporate Governance Network

- Fellow, Project Management Institute (PMI)
- Member, Chartered Governance Institute

❏ **Extra-Professional Activities & Interests**

- **Author**: *Roadmap to Non-Executive Directorship – The Essential Handbook*, a guide for aspiring board members and executives.
- **Mentor**: Actively mentor young professionals in corporate governance and leadership through the Director Mentorship Programme.
- **Public Speaking**: Regular speaker at industry conferences on topics such as governance, risk management, and sustainability.
- **Philanthropy**: Support education initiatives by serving as a trustee for [Organization], which focuses on improving access to quality education.

In my spare time, I enjoy exploring global innovation trends, traveling, and staying active through running and yoga. I am also passionate about property development and urban sustainability projects.

❏ **References**

Available upon request.

Here are some common interview questions for board positions, along with key questions you should ask during the interview. Use these to help you prepare effectively for the interview

Typical questions that may be asked at the board interview:

- Can you share your experience serving on boards or in governance roles?
- What inspired you to seek a position on our board?
- How do you view the board's role in ensuring effective governance and oversight?
- Can you give an example of when you worked with fellow board members to achieve a shared objective?
- What do you believe are the most pressing challenges facing our organization, and how would you address them?
- How familiar are you with our organization's mission, goals, and the challenges we face?
- What specific skills or expertise do you offer that would strengthen our board?
- Can you describe a situation where you faced a difficult decision as a board member? How did you handle it?
- How do you balance competing interests and perspectives when making strategic decisions?
- How do you manage conflicts of interest within a board setting?
- Can you highlight a recent industry trend or development that you find particularly relevant to our organization?
- How proficient are you in key areas such as stakeholder engagement, strategy development, and risk management?

Some typical questions that you should ask during the board interview:

- What is the company's long-term strategy, and how does the board contribute to its success?
- Where do you see skill gaps within the board or executive team that need to be addressed to achieve strategic goals?
- How are diversity, equity, and inclusion (DEI) or Environmental, Social, and Governance (ESG) integrated into the company's strategic agenda?
- What steps is the board taking to manage succession planning and ensure leadership continuity for sustainable growth?
- How does the board monitor and address underperformance, both at the executive level and among board members?
- What is the process for identifying and managing risks, and how does the board ensure adequate risk oversight?
- Can you describe the board's approach to corporate governance and regulatory compliance?
- How does the board engage with key stakeholders such as shareholders, employees, and the wider community?
- How does the board stay informed about emerging trends and industry disruptions that may impact the business?

www.ingramcontent.com/pod-product-compliance
Ingram Content Group UK Ltd.
Pitfield, Milton Keynes, MK11 3LW, UK
UKHW031324080125
4017UKWH00040B/280